DON'T FALL THROUGH
THE CRACKS!

Sid Sanghvi finally came to accept the ugly truths about the traditional education model when he was a second year college student in the US. Born and brought up in Mumbai, he attended many reputed schools around the world and experienced how teachers imparted knowledge. The patterns and flaws he observed during these years inspired him to write this book and help others become aware of the defects of the education system.

As an aspiring polymath and a lover of learning, he also writes blog posts on a wide range of topics covering philosophy, psychology, finance, science, technology, and history.

Visit sidsanghvi.com to learn more about the author.

DON'T FALL THROUGH THE CRACKS!

SID SANGHVI

RUPA

Published by
Rupa Publications India Pvt. Ltd 2021
7/16, Ansari Road, Daryaganj
New Delhi 110002

Sales centres:
Allahabad Bengaluru Chennai
Hyderabad Jaipur Kathmandu
Kolkata Mumbai

Copyright © Sid Sanghvi 2021
Cover art and illustrations: House of Awe

ISBN: 978-93-5333-944-9

First impression 2021

10 9 8 7 6 5 4 3 2 1

The moral right of the author has been asserted.

Contents

Introduction   *ix*

PART 1

THE PAST

1. Who we are   3

2. Once upon a time…   5

3. The next big things   10

4. The transition   12

5. Education for all?   14

6. We need more of them!   17

PART 2

THE PRESENT

7. So, what exactly is education today?   25

8. Exposing the cracks   28

9. Our Pre-Adult Years   29

10. Our Young Adult Years   43

11. What is college?   45

12. What was college?   47

13. Why is college so expensive?   53

14. So…how did we get here?   66

15. What has college become?   100

16. All Our Years   127

PART 3
THE FUTURE

17. Now what?   171

18. What should I do?   177

Epilogue   215

Acknowledgments   218

Notes & References   219

Introduction

It is of utmost importance for you, the reader, to be aware of the following: the contents of this book are based on fact, and the matters discussed are urgent. In writing this book, my goal is not to make it an academic resource or a technical research report, but to provide a bird's-eye view of the macro landscape of education in a comprehensible manner.

Have I reached out to any professionals within the education system? No. This is only because *most* professionals are not robust sources. They will not help one understand either what is happening today or the direction in which we are headed. The change—more importantly, the skyrocketing rate of change—that has taken place over the short span of a couple of generations is hard to fathom... for anyone.

You see, we humans are inherently linear thinkers. We have a seemingly innate disability of accurately predicting the relationship between the vast expanse of time and what can manifest within it. Evolving over millions of years on the plains of Africa, it was an anomaly for major change to take place within a single lifetime. Life, for the most part, was static. Resulting in the tendency of older human minds to settle into fixed ways of looking at the world and be satisfied with it. But this fixity not only restricts one from looking at the now without any preconceptions, but also severely handicaps the visualization of what could be.

This is why IBM did not believe in the personal computer. This is why Blackberry did not believe in the iPhone. This is why Blockbuster passed on Netflix. This is why Kodak did not believe in the digital camera. And, I'm not surprised.

For 99 per cent of human existence, our predisposition of looking at the world purely through the lens of the past was at the cutting edge of our understanding of what is, and what could be. Not anymore. Today, because of the accelerating rate of change, the best way of understanding what could be is, of course, by being aware of the past; but one must also look at the world objectively and not be satisfied by the accomplishments of previous generations.

Interestingly, more often than not, the type of person that fits both these criteria happens to be someone who would not have been alive to see the world fifty, twenty or even ten years ago. For this reason, those who are *currently* experiencing the education system or have just escaped from its predatory clutches, tend to be a much better source for our understanding of this matter. That said, I will provide you with one piece of information about myself. At the time of writing this sentence, I am twenty years of age and in the last month of my third year of college.

Throughout my life, I have been blessed with the opportunity to attend a variety of well-reputed schools. This has given me a front-row seat to observe not only the quality of education provided by institutions with the most exorbitant price tags, but also its effects on a great number of people. What I have seen, and very recently internalized, is nothing short of what I would describe as: a fictitious story presented as fact, and obfuscated beyond the scope of the person whom it affects the most.

Nonetheless, the very circumstance of my youth may be a pill too hard to swallow for some, given the nature and magnitude of the topics discussed. To those, consider this:

The following is straight from *ourworldindata.org*:

The Flynn effect describes the phenomenon that over time average IQ scores have been increasing in all countries since the turn of the twentieth century (the earliest point in time for which data is available). The change in IQ scores has been approximately three IQ points per decade. One major implications of this trend is that an average individual alive today would have an IQ of 130 by the standards of 1910, making them more intelligent than 98% of the population at that time. Equivalently, an individual alive in 1910, would have an IQ of 70 by today's standards, a score that would be low enough to be considered intellectually disabled in the modern world.[1]

My objective in providing this reference is to neither call myself a genius nor claim that IQ should be the only measure of intelligence, but to support the fact that age should not be a determinant of the relevance of what is discussed.

On a more opinionated note, it is myopic to believe wisdom and age are mutually inclusive. I suspect the archetype of the 'ignorant youth' came into being only after generations were made to yield their innate curiosities to an arbitrary standard of culture—best encapsulated by the letters A, B, C, D, and, of course, F. Suffice to say, wisdom does not arrive by making a simple trip around the sun. Anyone who remains idle for decades on end, with no desire to seek out the missing pieces of the puzzle that is the mind—either through the external world or by introspection—will not be wise, just old. My friend, do not mistake age for experience, for the mind can accrue experience beyond the measure of time by the measure of understanding.

However, I must acknowledge the truth in the same archetype. The positive correlation between age and wisdom is not only very real, but also must not be undermined. We, the youth, must not turn a blind eye to fact. The mere passage of time allows for the accumulation of more experiences, thus, more learning. Even though age shouldn't be seen as an untraversable barrier, we must make peace with the fact that the learning delta created by additional time is one too great to close in its entirety. That said, the dichotomy of the 'ignorant youth' and 'wise elderly' is false. It is not black and white; at least not as much as people—more so in conservative cultures—assume it to be. Especially in today's day and age, where this delta can be greatly minimized by relentless exposure to information from the virtually infinite sources that we have access to.

Personally, over the short twenty years that I have spent on this planet, what I have come to value most is Time—a misunderstood commodity when in our possession, and one that enslaves us when it's all too late. Therefore, my objective with this book is twofold: (1) To make you aware of pressing issues, those that potentially affect all of mankind, in a simple manner.* (2) To make the time you spend on this book, time well spent.

Lastly, it is my humble request that you hold on to any judgment, critiques, opinions, etc. until you have read the book in its entirety. If you do reach the very end, and find that what you have read is a blatant effort at spreading misinformation, then please, I invite you to throw it in the trash, light it on fire, and post a video of it online for the whole world to witness.

---

*Even though the content of this book is applicable to all education systems and learners worldwide, many examples used are from the American education system. This is only because it is what most of the world's education systems are modeled on.

Part 1

The Past

Rabindranath Tagore

'Don't limit a child to your own learning,
for he was born in another time.'

1
____

Who we are

What is one non-physiological characteristic that distinguishes humankind from the rest of the animate world?

Take a second, think on it.

Complex language? Large-scale cooperation? Consciousness or self-awareness? Abstract thought? Irrational hubris?

All of these are fair answers. But for now, since the privilege of determining the correct answer is mine, I must reject them (along with the others unmentioned). The distinguishable feature I allude to is our *aptitude for erudition*. In other words, we have a knack for learning; that too, a whole lot more than we—every single one of us—are led to believe.

Homo sapiens are the *only* known animate instance that exemplifies this potential to absorb, retain and utilize such great amounts of information about their perceived reality. We understand, and this simple fact is no trivial matter!

It is your aptitude for erudition that allows you to read these words right now. It is the reason you have clothes that have been spun halfway across the world, purchased from the comfort of your home and then delivered within the week. It is why you have more computational power in the palm of your hand than that which once sent man to the moon. It is why we have art that gives us goosebumps. It is why more people today die from eating too much as opposed to too little. It is why almost everything we deem as necessities exists in the first place.

It's clear that learning—super learning, in our case—is pretty damn important, so it pays to know what's happening with it in today's world. Are we leveraging this superpower effectively, or are we systematically depriving future generations of the potential it may offer?

That said, before we begin, we're going to take a quick detour. Let us go back in time to gain some perspective of where exactly this superpower comes from, and learn how it has helped us thus far.

2

Once upon a time…

S oon after our beautiful planet took the shape we are familiar with today—vast oceans with chunks of land sandwiched in between—it took only a couple of cosmic moments for the first signs of life to emerge.[1] Fast-forward to about 2.5 million years ago, and the first humans appeared—*Homo habilis*. Even though these guys could only use crude tools made of stone, this alone exemplified a learning of several orders of magnitude greater than any species that had come before.[2]

We attribute this incredible jump in learning to the human brain—the most complex structure we know of, even today. We're not sure how and/or why the brain evolved, especially because big brains come at a heavy price—they need a LOT of energy.

The initial increase in brain capacity occurred probably due to reasons such as the need of depth perception in vision and navigating social hierarchies. However, to explain the next phase of brain growth, there are a plethora of hypotheses. Some say it was due to the need for complex language, required in order to maintain relationships as groups got larger. Some say it could have been the increase in the quantity of meat in our diet, or the excess energy freed up by cooking instead of digesting raw food. And some suggest the consumption of psychedelic plants triggered the formation of new neural pathways over hundreds of thousands of years. We can never test any of these theories, so the exact reason may never be known. It could be any one of them, all of them or none of them.[3] Whatever it was, the benefits of a bigger brain far outweighed the cost needed to sustain it.

One of these benefits was *Collective Learning*—the ability of a species to retain more information within a single generation than is lost by the next. Think of it as the aptitude for erudition at a species-wide level. Collective learning is the same fundamental concept that we homo sapiens have used to get to where we are now, and will continue to utilize as we move forward.

Over the next two-million years or so, several other human species like *Homo erectus, Homo brigansus* and the *Neanderthals,* developed the first systematic use of fire, spears and other composite tools. Approximately 250,000 years ago, we appeared.

If we consider this advancement from a bird's-eye view: it took life billions of years to attain a sliver of structured learnability (the emergence of apes), then tens-of-millions of years for the rise of *Homo habilis,* another two-million to harness fire and more complex tools, and, lastly, only a quarter millennium to get to where we are today.[4]

This makes two things clear; learning is our thing, and the rate at which we learn is only speeding up.

Of course, this doesn't mean we can just sit back and wait for it to happen. Learning wasn't—and no matter how far technology has come—still isn't, a passive phenomenon. We must always be completely present in the acquisition of knowledge. Confucius knew this a-millennium-and-a-half ago: 'Learning without thought is labor lost.'

Now, this precept is deceivingly difficult; it rarely ever materializes in real-life. When learning something new, we often think we are trying our level-best, investing a significant amount of quality time, and yet learning eludes us. This is because we naively disregard the future we wish to create through this acquisition of knowledge. In other words, a necessary prerequisite for any learning is the presence of an adequate incentive for sustained self-motivation—we need a 'why,' and a *relevant* 'why' at that. We internalize knowledge differently when we can clearly visualize the outlook that we want to avoid, and know that it *will inevitably happen* if we don't figure out how to make sense of the knowledge we wish to acquire.

> If we know why we are learning and if the reason fits our needs
> as we perceive them, we will learn quickly and deeply.[5]

Malcolm Knowles spoke these words, way back in 1973. He rose to prominence due to his ideas about *andragogy*—the art and science of teaching adults. Whereas andragogy puts emphasis on the learner, *pedagogy*—what is practiced in our schools—puts emphasis on the teacher. Think back to your days in school: who decided what, when and how to learn? Chances are, it was anyone but you.

On the other hand, andragogy puts the responsibility of learning on the learner; since adults don't *have* to learn, they choose to. The irony is that all learning is andragogical. Pedagogy is useless if it doesn't succeed in executing andragogical principles. In other words, if a teacher doesn't manage to make the student desire to learn by themselves, especially for subjects with no *explicit* utility in daily life, no substantial learning will take place.

According to Erik Kandel, a Nobel Prize-winning neuroscientist, learning is only but a series of physical changes within our brain; when we learn, nerve cells *literally* grow. Think of it as your brain going to the gym. Just as regular utilization of a muscle group makes it grow stronger, the more active a neuron is, the more physical connections it develops with surrounding cells. This allows it to not only pass messages faster and more articulately, but also store more information. Learning is nothing but a function of the number and size of these connections.[6]

Point is, learning entails a lot of chemical and electrical work, which requires energy to be channeled in a fruitful direction. The 'energy' part of the equation comes from our physical bodies, but the direction can only be fulfilled by us, the learner. If we don't know why we're learning, no learning will take place, even when substantial energy is utilized. This is why school is tiring! We're told to learn *all* this stuff to get good grades, but it quickly becomes evident that passing grades can be achieved with minimal effort. So then we ask, 'Why are we being made to go through this incredibly tiresome process of learning?' Based on what is taught today, there's seldom a good answer, so we're left with no valid *'why'*. And so, we learn little, while still returning home from school looking like we haven't slept in days.

For our ancestors, this was no obstacle—their *why* was *to not die*. And they did what was necessary to achieve that goal. The miracle was that in the presence of this incentive, the ability to understand and improve also transpired. We could make sense of what could kill us and actively created, to decrease its chances. Talk about revolutionary!

Relative to our biological history, formal education is an extremely new phenomenon. During the time of hunter-gatherers, learning *was* living (even today, albeit not as explicit). A mother taught her child to climb a tree when the child was hungry and the lesson was unmistakably related to reducing the child's discomfort. Nonetheless, for the majority of this period, children learned through self-exploration and play,[7] both which are triggered by innate curiosity. Even today, a child's curiosity is a phenomenon unparalleled in any other walks of life, and for good reason—they have so much more to learn! Ironically, back then, our species took advantage of this to a much greater effect than we do now.

Now, when I speak of *education*, what most people think of is *schooling*; something done *to* children *by* adults.

The truth is, education long predates school or any other form of structured learning. For the majority of human existence, the responsibility of education lay in the hands of the child, not the adult. Today, we feel that if a child is not systematically made to acquire certain information, they won't *ever* do so. This could not be further from the truth. Genetically, we are all still hunter-gatherers. We have been so for the majority of human existence and will continue to be so for the near future, as biological evolution takes millions of years to perform a software update.[8]

This means that children are biologically predisposed to take charge of their own education! Back in the day, a child learned by using curiosity as their guide—this is childhood as nature intended it to be. Children aren't made to simply do as they are told, but to do as others do. They excel at imitating, not following instruction. This was the foundation of hunter-gatherer parenting and education philosophy. It worked wonders. Children were allowed to follow their own curiosities in the pursuit to gain knowledge, and were trusted to contribute to the tribe's economy when they acquired the requisite skills to do so. This doesn't mean the group did not aid in a child's growth—quite the contrary—a child simply directed his own learning. The adults and other children were resources—if and when any were needed.[9]

Most interestingly, because of the liberty accorded to children, learning at its most pure form was indistinguishable from play.

This is not a happy coincidence. It is by design—it had to be that way. If it wasn't pleasurable, youngsters wouldn't learn. And if they didn't learn and hone their skills, survival would be a long shot in the cutthroat reality of the wild. To fail to learn was to die, making *play* a very strong survival mechanism.

3

The next big things

When it comes to technology, *the next big thing* is as inevitable as death and taxes. The difference is that during the days of our ancient ancestors, *the next big thing* came every once in a blue moon. With each new breakthrough having arguably more of an impact on society, than that of the faster processor or better camera resolution on the latest smartphone.

The first example of this is language.

As time forged along, language not only radically improved the efficiency with which people shared complex ideas, but also made society increasingly specialized. This was because children weren't constrained; they did more than mimic their parents. They could actively learn from others when time permitted. Thus, emerged the first primitive forms of the apprenticeship education model. This was huge! (1) Now, the responsibility of education didn't solely lie in the hands of the parent, and (2) it laid the groundwork for a philosophy that is still prevalent today—the notion that education is done *by* the adult *to* the child.

The next big thing was agriculture. The advent of agriculture completely changed the way we played the game of life. Although many attribute the seeds of our modern education system to have been planted during the Industrial Revolution, I believe they were sown here.

We don't really know for sure how agriculture spread across ancient society, but it represented a monumental shift in human activity. Before this, every animal adapted to fit into the environment. Now, for the first time ever, we adapted the environment to suit our needs.

Agriculture freed us from the constant pursuit of food; unbeknown to us then, this would prove to be a double-edged sword. With agriculture, a small number of people could grow more than enough food for the entire tribe, thereby allowing not only the group to grow larger, but also giving its members the room to pursue a variety of tasks.[1] However, even as more food was produced, freedom was sacrificed.[2]

In other words, where hunter-gatherers sought out food that grew naturally (don't forget the abundance and thrill of nature), agriculture forced people to remain close to where their crops were planted. Requiring long hours of unskilled, mundane and repetitive labour. Everything that *just so* happens, when coerced, can be done by a child. As the size of families started growing rapidly (and unsustainably), the life of a child gradually changed from the free exploration of interests, to working in the fields and taking care of an increasing number of sickly at home. In other words, childhood transformed from the exploration of the world to servitude of the family.[3]

4

The transition

Over time, socioeconomic status became as real as the need for water to sustain life. By the turn of the Common Era, the stringent class system in the East and feudalism in the West, effectively made childhood an immense bottleneck for any population to grow.[1] Families had several children because they knew that chances were slim for any one to reach adulthood. Of course, disease and human conflict also caused this bottleneck, but a less commonly mentioned culprit is simple child exploitation. Here's an excerpt from a 14th/15th century document quoting a French count:

> Choose a boy servant as young as seven or eight... this boy should be beaten until he has a proper dread of failing to carry out his master's orders.[2]

This is just the tip of the iceberg, but it does give perspective.

One would think that as society progressed into the early Industrial Era, with an increased understanding of how the world worked, the value of childhood would increase. Unfortunately, that wasn't the case. With the emergence of industrial production and the consequent accumulation of wealth, the ability to move through social classes improved. But, the life of a child went from bad to worse. Like any other employee, children were forced into dangerous, congested, filthy and dark workplaces. By the mid-1800s, more than half of all New England factory employees were kids aged 7-18. Working, on average, from sunrise to 8 p.m., six days a week.[3] Disease, starvation, equipment failure and exhaustion killed thousands each year.

From the emergence of agriculture, to as close to a century ago (and some might argue it still exists today), the objective of a child's education was the systematic transformation of their desires into obedience. A good child was one that suppressed the urge to play, explore and try new things, especially when it contradicted the orders of the ~~masters~~ adults.

5

Education for all?

As the bold arrow of technology marched on, the need for child labour in industry declined. Consequently (or maybe not), the ideology of *education as a birth right* quickly emerged in religious and secular communities alike. Finally, a hint of progress.

But wait!

The right thing for the wrong reasons can be just as bad as the wrong thing in the first place. And this is exactly what happened. Even though institutionalized education was sold as a birth right, each institution had its own agenda.

Somewhere along the line, education became a morally acceptable manner through which one could propagate their ideology and beliefs. Religious bodies saw education as a path to salvation; political leaders saw it as a path to create better national servants; and employers saw it as a path to create better employees. Education was, in actuality, *indoctrination.* The world was taught as an already understood phenomenon, even though that was (and still is) far from the truth. The value of self-exploration (something the hunter-gatherers understood over millennia ago) was yet to be realized.[1]

Slowly, similar to how working is seen as the responsibility of an adult, going to school was seen as the responsibility of a child.[2] Here is where things get sticky. Now, children were handed a moral obligation—they must remember things that they, for lack of a better word, didn't give a f**k about. On top of that, children would be punished if they failed to do so.

The perfect formula to brainwash young humans, generation after generation.

This indoctrination catalysed two very dangerous beliefs that are still prevalent today: (1) the perception of rote memory as intellect, and (2) the desires of a child, and education, are two mutually exclusive activities.[3] So, when a child forgot that *one* mathematical theorem, the obvious explanation was that the student didn't care, or didn't try hard enough. A physical beating was necessary to make sure it didn't happen again. Punishment was seen as an intrinsic part of the process. One teacher in Germany kept a record of all the *educating* he had done:

> 911,527 blows with a rod, 124,010 blows with a cane, 20,989 taps with a ruler, 136,715 blows with the hand, 10,235 blows to the mouth, 7,905 boxes on the ear, and 1,118,800 blows on the head.[4]

Things are a bit different today. Yes, we have reduced the physical dangers present and managed to integrate a more diverse range of subjects in school. But, the same basic principles of education persist. Them being:

1. Learning cannot happen naturally, so children must be forced to do so. Resulting in school being mandatory, and attending it a child's responsibility.
2. The school determines what to teach based on an ideology intended to be propagated through the curriculum. Today that is: college is the best path for everyone.
3. Learning is hard work and not a pleasurable activity.
4. If a child cannot *put in the work*, something must be done about it—before it was physical beatings, today it's pills.
5. Quantity and quality of learning received can be boiled down to a letter or number.

As you can see, we humans have created an artificial world, one we cannot differentiate from reality. Consequently, childhood is not only defined by the school's requirements, but also eroded from experiencing the value of learning—the greatest crime of all, in my opinion.

I know the picture I've painted seems dystopian. All this probably didn't strike you the last time you visited a school. Of course, it didn't! That would be bad for the school's business. The problem is so obfuscated that most teachers genuinely believe what they're doing is the right thing. I suspect this is due to them accepting the system for how it is. And I don't blame them, most of my teachers had good intentions. The issue is systemic. No amount of lip service to *holistic pedagogy, interdisciplinary curriculum,* or whatever jargon is used can provide a solution.

Instead, we should focus on creating an environment that stimulates and satisfies a student's *own* curiosity. We should focus on making learning synonymous with the child's interests. We should figure out how to create the best environment to facilitate self-learning, because, in the real world, that's the only type of learning that can exist.

Still uncertain? Let me try to make it more relatable. If you are a parent/student/teacher, do you ever remember hearing, 'finish your work, then play'? What about the proverb, 'all work and no play makes Jack a dull boy?'

Therein lies the issue!

The (incorrect) underlying philosophies of the education system has forced Jack to pick between play and work. The one thing the student takes away from school, if anything at all, is that play, something that results in enjoyment, is by definition different from learning.

It took me twenty years to realize that learning can be fun! That it can be indistinguishable from play. It can be whatever I want it to be. In fact, *it only works when I want to do it.* And I consider myself lucky, most go through their entire lives without coming to this realization.

6

We need more of them!

I nertia is an incredibly strong force in every facet of reality. It's why we don't have to worry about the Earth suddenly moving away from the Sun. It's what makes habit such a potent means to accomplish, well, anything. But unfortunately, inertia is also what makes things seem inevitable. In other words, the fact that something has existed a particular way allows us to rationalize its worth. Whereas, in reality, some things are nothing but mere human inventions. One example being today's education system. Point is, it's a dangerous practice to default to an opinion or rationale just because everyone else follows it. And the first step to avoiding this oversight is to understand how *a* status quo became *the* status quo in the first place.

The age-based batch system that we are all aware of, the one where children are grouped based on year of birth, dates back to the industrial revolution. It was in the late 1700s early 1800s, when Prussia (modern-day Germany) conceived and implemented a system that is known today as *The Factory School Model*.[1]

For its time, this was revolutionary!

It allowed for education to take place in a scalable, affordable and efficient manner. Later, in the mid-1800s, Horace Mann, an American education reformer, took notice of this model and brought it to the United States.[2]

By 1870, public education in the USA had become mainstream.

However, all throughout the country, the subject material taught, the level of difficulty, student proficiency and other educational standards varied greatly. Consequently, the unpredictability of an applicant's academic background became a growing issue for universities; they couldn't accurately assess the academic level of an incoming student. In response, the National Education Association decided that all schooling prior to that of college had to be standardized. And so, in 1892, emerged the 'Committee of Ten'. This group of ten men put together a plan dictating the learning requirements for America's children. They decided on twelve years of pre-university education, divided into primary, middle and high school, and set standards for the material taught.[3] Thus began the standardized system of education we use all around the world today.

Little has changed in the last century. The basic principles still remain the same, and this is a problem. Why? To answer that, let's first take a closer look at the education system adopted by the Prussians— what it was and how it came to be.

Around the late 1700s, King Frederick William II of Prussia officially declared that a child's education was the responsibility of the state, as opposed to that of the church or parent. Intriguingly, some say this was due to Prussia's defeat against Napoleon; the rationale being that the defeat was caused by the soldiers' inability to follow direct orders and tendency to think for themselves.[4]

Whatever the reason, by the late 1830s, approximately 80 per cent of Prussian children were put into state-run mandatory schools.[5] The exposure of a large populace to knowledge was unheard of back then and is pretty impressive in its own right. But it was only possible because of a new education system known as, you guessed it, 'The Factory School Model'. It was an eight-year program, not only consisting of subjects critical to the early industrial world such as reading, writing and arithmetic, but also one which strictly pushed forward the idea of duty to the nation, discipline, respect for authority

Products of assembly line education

and the importance of following orders.

The end goal of this system was to instill deep social obedience in every citizen. They aimed to develop absolute loyalty to the Crown and train young men for the military and bureaucracy. Here's where things get eye-opening.

One of the main advocates for this system was the Prussian philosopher, Johann Gottlieb Fichte. He, along with others, used concepts from earlier prominent figures such as Jean-Jacques Rousseau and John Locke to qualify the system as *scientific*. They defined (for the child) what was to be learned, what to think about and how long to think about it. They believed that to avoid chaos and operate an efficiently-functioning society, it was essential for most citizens to be unable to make sense of the available information.[6] Why else would closely interlinked bodies of knowledge be balkanized into fragments referred to as 'subjects'? This was a system that mass-produced sheep that catalyzed rapid national growth without proportional risk of civil unrest. To quote Johann Fichte,

> The schools must fashion the person, and fashion him in such a way that he simply cannot will otherwise than what you wish him to will.[7]

He was also quoted saying,

> Education should aim at destroying free will, so that, after pupils have left school, they shall be incapable, throughout the rest of their lives, of thinking or acting otherwise than as their schoolmasters would have wished.[8]

Fichte's philosophies, which included expressive advocacy for anti-Semitism, went on to be a strong influencer in the rise of Nazism. And it was the no-questions-asked type of loyalty to the nation that sparked Hitler's rise to power.

This is the genesis of the education system that exists all over the world today, in some form or the other. Knowing this, it's unsurprising why the origin of our education system isn't as widely discussed. It was never designed to be effective for student learning. It was never designed to make the learner be the best he can be. It was always designed to aid the agendas of people with influence.

Whether or not the Prussian system was designed with the sole purpose of indoctrination, it severely restricted free, creative, independent and critical thought. Of course, today, the only obvious change is that children are not strictly raised to be soldiers or servants of the nation. But, as I've already mentioned, the core principles remain the same.

With that, we come to the end of Part 1.

In summary, we've seen the ancestry of the education system, its evolution from the time of hunter-gatherers, and looked into the roots of today's philosophies of education. In Part 2, we take a deep-dive into the system that exists today—examining how it works, its benefits and drawbacks, and so on.

The Present

Dr. Nassim Taleb

'Education is an institution that has been growing
without external stressors; eventually the thing will collapse.'

7

So, what exactly is education today?

Formal education can be divided, for the most part, into two distinct categories: K-12 and Higher Education. The former being kindergarten to high school, and the latter being college/university.

A stereotypical example of the education process would go somewhat like this:

1. A child is ushered into kindergarten at age 4-5.
2. The child moves up grade levels, year-by-year, by attaining the minimum score required.
3. This continues linearly up until high school (9th grade). Now, it is time to prepare for college. The child must invest hours in extra-curricular activities, in addition to achieving the highest grades in academics. This is to show colleges that the student is not only book smart, but also *well-rounded.*
4. About two years later, another college requirement is introduced— standardized tests. Now, test preparation is added to the juggling act, alongside academics and extracurriculars.
5. Finally, around age eighteen, it is time for college!
6. Assuming the traditional four-year program, the first two years are spent taking a set of mandatory common classes, irrespective of their course of study. And during the following two years, students take classes based on their career goals. However, all throughout, additional classes must also be taken as per their interests.

7. Hooray! The student obtains their degree and has completed their educational journey (unless the plan is to go to graduate school). The college graduate is now more valuable in the employer's eye, as the degree is proof of their competence.

On the surface, this seems like an innocuous process. But alas, the devil is in the details.

Now, before I can shine some light on the cracks, it is critical that we agree upon the following: the sole overarching purpose of the entire education system is to prepare students for the uncertainties of the future, to develop their faculties so that they can produce for society, and to make them the best adults they can be.

That said, by no means am I saying that the current education system is the worst it has ever been. Quite the contrary. I genuinely believe that the initial reasons for the transition to today's practices were noble and the right ones.

K-12 does incredibly well at introducing a whole array of subjects, as opposed to the one-dimensional Reading, Writing and Arithmetic; that extracurriculars are valued at all, and that time is reserved for physical exercise, are both beautiful and sensible ideas; and for those determined to pursue further studies, some high school curricula prepare students in a fool-proof manner. As for higher education, the concept is one that is very close to my heart. An institution, more importantly, a safe environment, dedicated to not only one's voluntary pursuit of knowledge but also the free exchange of ideas is one of the greatest inventions of all mankind; the immense variety of facilities and people alone can present a very rich learning culture and strong positive feedback loops; alumni, too, provide a lot of value as they opens doors for students that would have otherwise been impossible.

As a lover of learning, I must also confess that even though subjects like Calculus, Quadratic Equations, Pythagoras Theorem, Plant Biology, Electromagnetism, etc. are useless to most in real life, the fact that students are exposed to them is something that I wholeheartedly advocate. After all, these subjects represent the epitome of human achievement; they describe the truths of our universe. It would be a crime to steal one's opportunity to be aware of their own species' accomplishments that have allowed the world we live in today to exist.

Unfortunately—or fortunately—we are all humans, and as humans, we have a knack of never being satisfied. When something can be improved, it must be. And trust me, a lot can be improved in education today. To believe that the positives are all there are is delusional. I am confident people will wake up to the facts, sooner or later.

As the saying goes, 'You can fool all the people some of the time and some of the people all the time, but you cannot fool all the people all the time'.

I'm just trying to expedite the process.

8

Exposing the cracks

Now, let's get into the meat of everything we've spoken about thus far.

For easy comprehension, the following chapters are divided into three distinct categories: K-12, Higher Education and the entire Education System, respectively.

Before we begin, I will say this: yes, it is very easy to find niche arguments to deny individual claims I make, but it's important to keep in mind that my assertions are only directed at those institutions, people, phenomena, etc. that represent the numerical majority (unless stated otherwise). In today's radically interconnected world, it's nearly impossible to make claims that aren't subject to exceptions.

So if a contrary argument does pop up in your mind, ask yourself, 'does it change the truth of the overarching message being conveyed?'

If not, keep reading.

9

Our Pre-Adult Years

Youth—is often how this period of time is described. A blink-of-an-eye in life, where we are blessed with peak neurogenesis to best equip ourselves with knowledge essential to successfully manoeuvre through the world thrust upon us.

This is why I love the idea of K-12 Education. The collective effort to prepare our future generations, by giving them the foundation needed to be a functioning member of society, is a human accomplishment second to none. A place where one is exposed to the truths of our reality, can develop social skills that make society tick, receive the opportunity to feed their bubbling curiosity, and so much more.

But alas, much of what I just stated above does not exist in totality. The truth is bitter in spite of what we may believe (or wish to). Schools are definitely accomplishing these goals to a much better degree than before, but we're nowhere close to an acceptable standard. The primary issue plaguing our K-12 schools is that their prestige is derived from college placements. Now, even though I've simplified the matter into a single sentence, the resulting ripple effects have severe implications.

For many millennia, a child learned by doing something random, experiencing what happened thereafter, and repeating the action until it made sense (which leads to boredom, triggering the willingness to learn something new). This free, erratic, spontaneous, time-consuming and mistake-rampant process is how children are wired to learn. It takes a *lot* of energy, but as we know, this is no hurdle for children. Their inability is in channeling said energy into a single direction over long periods of time. Ironically, this is exactly how most K-12 education is structured. For twelve arduous years, *each year*, students are evaluated on some adult-created criteria of an adult-determined set of things.

The first issue is obvious, we have arbitrarily assigned time to learning. We, as a society, have come to accept that by a certain age we should have an understanding of certain things. Just for a second, stop and think about this—why is a child expected to know any specific set of things at any given point in time?

I'm not suggesting we shouldn't have thresholds.

For example, by the end of high school, students should definitely be aware of basic economics; or, if a student displays a clear biological inadequacy in cognition, then the necessary care should be taken. What I'm referring to is the more general K-12 material (Geometry, Literary Analysis, States of Matter, Trigonometry, Electromagnetism, etc.) and their introduction at specific grade levels. If a child in 8th grade is struggling with 6th grade Mathematics, what does this mean? According to our system, clear enough, the student is a bit slow. They must work harder; they are obviously falling behind. But what if the teacher is themselves failing to explain it in a manner that the student comprehends? What if they need to reinforce what they already know to be able to successfully apply their knowledge? What if all that's needed is simply more time?

This doesn't mean there's anything inherently wrong with the child. The accepted expected standard is one that we ourselves have created, but this doesn't make it correct. We seem to forget that every child is an individual, and enforcing conformity can easily have unintended consequences, often to their detriment.

For now, since the imposition of time to learning isn't exactly a direct consequence of the *college placement determining K-12 prestige* assertion, let's move on. The implications certainly don't end here, so a more thorough discussion is presented in Chapter 16.

After the nine-year struggle to forcefully embed information, children must start building their college applications. Now, additional evaluations are imposed, such as extracurricular activities and standardized tests, simply because colleges demand them. In turn, this process not only paints college as a *golden ticket* to one's future (which, as we'll see, is far from the truth), but also greatly overvalues college requirements. Here, another fallacy is propagated—rote memorization as a sign of intelligence.

The effectiveness of regurgitating not-fully-understood information makes rote memorization a very handy and efficient tool at achieving the highest scores. As employers know, this skill is seldom of any use in the real world. Conveniently, this is inconsequential to high schools as they aren't judged by where the child is in the long term, but only by the short-term metric of college placement.

As for standardized tests, their perceived value has become so unfathomably high that entire test-prep industries have spawned, resulting in pay-walls for low-income students as they cannot access the necessary classes to prepare for these tests. Unsurprisingly, research shows test-scores have a stronger correlation with family income than with student intelligence.[1] What I'm completely dumbfounded by is that society values these tests so much that we've become blind to the symptoms of toxicity staring right at us.

Attending these test-prep classes quickly reveals that the concepts being taught have little value in the real world. Here's an example: one of the most popular strategies taught in all test-prep classes is known as the *Process of Elimination*. Yes, it's extremely effective in procuring a high score, but one learns absolutely nothing! Assuming a student answers correctly, they are literally rewarded for not knowing what they were supposed to know. It is regarded as one of the most useful strategies to maximize scores, and I have to agree; I've used it many times and still do so in college today. But the fact remains, a method so vital to achieving high scores contributes so little to one's learning.

Now, it's important to note that my argument is not that standardized tests are inherently bad or useless. It's our overvaluation of them that's the problem. They can provide immense information about a candidate's competence, but it's no panacea. A good score is a good predictor of high levels of competence, but a low score may imply many things: low competence, low willingness to learn arbitrary information, low access to test preparation or a whole host of other conclusions. Some universities understand the false-positives of standardized tests and have reduced their weight while filtering for college applicants, but for the most part, our cultural perception of them has never been held in higher regard.

As for extracurricular activities—in theory, they seem to be a wonderful supplement to a child's growth. But this view quickly crumbles when they are considered a means to improve one's college application. This is so because only activities that can be verified are truly given importance. Being a member of the High School sports team or participation in a well-known science competition are valid activities, but spending countless hours playing a sport recreationally or watching science videos in your spare time are not. This category should be rightfully called, *Adult-directed Extracurricular Activities.* Suffice to say, a very powerful learning force is taken away when children feel coerced to do something in a specific way, different from how *they* want to do it.

Ironically, in the pursuit to differentiate, we've adopted a philosophy that does exactly the opposite! 'You should play a sport. You should pick up an instrument. You should join some club.' Do you see where I'm going with this? If we *design* kids to be the way we assume other people—in our case, admission officers—want them to be, inadvertently, they lose authenticity. And nobody has ever excelled in anything without authenticity.

Another consequence of worshipping college placements is the superficial increase in educational standards. Following this model, colleges have maximum leverage. At the core lies filtration; students must prove to possess a higher ability than the rest to be accepted. Naturally, a curriculum that sets the bar higher than the last will have greater capacity to filter. So, when colleges accept new curricula, K-12 institutions are quick to adopt the new *highest standard*—they have to, their business depends on it!

Point is, in the pursuit to set the bar higher, we universally gravitate towards making changes that increase the perceived rigour of the curriculum, without considering its ability to execute on the advertised standards. On paper it seems like it promotes greater learning but in reality, it only increases the disparity amongst students' grades, precisely which aids timely filtration.

What are these factors that increase perceived but not actual learning?

Well, for one, the large quantity of seemingly irrelevant topics studied. This claim should come as no surprise to those who have endured a decade or more of schooling, so let me double-down on its implications.

First, let's address the elephant in the room—the argument that the diverse array of subjects allows students to discover what they like. In my opinion, this holds woefully little water. *Discovery* requires exploration, and that is the last thing allowed in schools. There is one fixed curriculum; everyone learns the same thing at the same time. Worst of all, when a student finally chances upon a tangent they seem to be interested in, they're cut off in the name of lack of time. This undermines not only the process of discovery, but also tells students that what they want to do is a waste of time.

Moving on, it's important to understand that our brains have evolved to disregard information it considers irrelevant. *Forgetting,* for all the bad press it gets, is one of the most important functions of our brain. This helps in understanding why students tend to forget a good chunk of material when returning to school after a break.[2] Students constantly face the uphill battle against *fadeout*—the tendency of forgetting knowledge seldom used.[3] So, for example, when we're taught the Pythagorean Theorem, and neither understand why we're investing time and energy into it nor use it out of class, we tend to forget it. Later, when we experience outcry from authority figures, we're constantly reminded that if we don't do what is told we won't get into a good college or get a good job. Now, kids aren't stupid. When they go home to their parents, and see first-hand that the majority of what is taught is not utilized in daily life, it gives rise to cognitive dissonance, which inevitably results in detriment to the student's learning.

Sure, when kids are in middle school they might not see the value in some topics that are, in fact, useful, but what about high school? Let's take mathematics as an example. Assuming a firm grasp on the concepts, if algebra and geometry did not leave the student in awe and wanting to learn more, I can bet money that calculus won't change a thing. I'm not undermining the value of mathematics as a subject, instead I'm suggesting that if a student is clearly not going to pursue niche mathematics down the line, wouldn't a better use of time be to allow the student to gain knowledge on the mathematical aspects of life that we know for a fact they will encounter? Say, financial literacy?

Another factor we adore is time spent in school—this is so true that we've gone ahead and made it mandatory. It is literally breaking the law to not go. Sure, home-schooling is an option, but it serves a very niche population; it takes a huge toll on parents, one that many can't afford, so traditional schooling remains mainstream. Here, things get a bit sticky. In principle, mandatory schooling is well-intentioned, but reality doesn't care about your intentions.

The first problem of mandatory schooling is that it blatantly undermines curiosity—our innate drive to learn.

Humans come into the world as quintessential learning machines.

In a mere four years, children learn to walk, run, climb, speak, understand, relate—all because it's genetically encoded. It's not that they want to do it, it's that they *have to want* to do it. Then we must ask again, if children are designed to learn instinctively, why do they not enjoy the place designed to do exactly that? Well, beyond the drive to learn, we have the drive to be free.

Need I state the obvious?

Naturally, we rebel. We fight back. We try to make our oppressors miserable. In which case, retaliation abounds—detentions, parents are brought in, the attacks become personal. In these conditions, it becomes very hard to accomplish anything productive, let alone learn—probably one of the most mentally demanding tasks one can do. Sometimes, in an effort to bring back stability, we're told all this is for our own good. It is our responsibility—our job, our work—to do what is told; most of us concede, resenting every second nonetheless.

Curiosity doesn't magically disappear when we start school. This drive to learn is systematically extinguished by compulsory schooling. Einstein summed it up best:

> It is nothing short of a miracle that the modern methods of instruction have not yet entirely strangled the holy curiosity of inquiry; for this delicate plant, aside from stimulation, stands mainly in need of freedom; without this it goes to wreck and ruin without fail. It is a very grave mistake to think that the enjoyment of seeing and searching can be promoted by means of coercion and a sense of duty.[4]

Elsewhere, he also said:

> One had to cram all this stuff into one's mind, whether one liked it or not. This coercion had such a deterring effect that, after I had passed the final examination, I found the consideration of any scientific problems distasteful to me for an entire year[5]

Let that sink in. In another universe, *the institution that promotes knowledge* could itself be the reason Einstein didn't, arguably, make the biggest scientific breakthrough of our time.

The next consequence of mandatory schooling is that it ironically undermines the concept of learning.

I want to begin by drawing your attention to the fact that the majority of K-12 learning is dependent on a student's family atmosphere at home. Out of the glut of research, one large study done at the University of Michigan concluded that the single strongest predictor of better student learning and fewer behavioural problems is not time spent at school or doing homework, but the frequency and duration of family meals.[6] This shouldn't come as a surprise. Family time is where children are free from the never-ending storm of social media, values are instilled, the sense of isolation eradicated, and support made explicit. It allows for the necessary social and mental foundations to be laid for actual learning to even have a shot.

So, why have we devised and accepted a system which doesn't allow students to take a week-long break from school, say, for a family holiday, without facing setbacks?

The reality is that students stand to fall behind even if they miss a single day of school, thus making families play second-fiddle to the curriculum; all because we've incrementally increased schooling hours under the false pretence that more time devoted to this cause will result in greater learning.

Another factor that is closely tied to family time is that of homework.

This is a sensitive topic for many as the predominant belief is that the more homework assigned, the more the student learns. Unfortunately, as a stand-alone measure, it's useless to predict *future student performance.*

Homework is a concept that should exist as a last resort—not a staple. It becomes necessary when inadequate learning happens during the school day. (Simply trimming the fat amongst curricula can easily drive down the need for it.) Nevertheless, the correct question isn't 'how much homework?' but 'why homework?' Some say, to develop a sense of responsibility, accountability, independence, time management, etc. These are all fair arguments. But the key rebuttal here is: 1) the work done at home must be discussed in class (which rarely happens). At most, it's corrected for right-and-wrong and promptly forgotten. 2) These traits aren't exclusively granted by homework. People demonstrated them long before the advent of homework.

Instead, what we see today is an ever-increasing quantity of homework that not only restricts family time, but also takes a toll on the student's mental health.[7]

Moving on, let's discuss cheating.

Mandatory schooling's main premise is that students must learn; their entire life depends on it. However, once in the system, it doesn't take a genius to figure out that all that matters is the grade. This sets the foundation for a lifetime of cynicism towards formal education as the rationale given was a lie—as long as you get the grade, nobody cares about how much you learn. School, then, becomes a game, one that students didn't choose to play. A game where they don't have a say as to what its purpose is, what is considered winning and what is considered fair play. Under such circumstances, it's difficult to respect the rules. Moreover, one quickly realizes that the rules of fair play are arbitrary; they have very little to do with learning. If one makes a summary sheet of the information and looks at it during the test, they have cheated. If another makes the same sheet, memorizes it and then forgets everything after the test, they haven't done anything wrong. If one student copies another's writing, it's cheating. If another does the same, changes a few phrases and alters the structure, then it isn't. Unsurprisingly, cheating is now commonplace.

- On anonymous questionnaires, about 95 per cent of students admitted to some degree of cheating; about 70 per cent admitted to repeated acts of blatant cheating, like copying entire tests, plagiarism, etc.[8]
- I can attest to the above.

ഗ

By cheating, you're only ruining your own education—that's what they say. But this is only valid if: (1) the material learned by not cheating is more valuable than what you did with the time saved, or (2) the material learned is more valuable than the grade. In most cases, both criteria don't stand scrutiny. Usually, the time saved by cheating is used to study a subject that the student really cares about (a consequence of the overvalued grade). This is also why it's a faulty assumption to think that only 'bad' students cheat. Increasingly, students at the opposite end of the spectrum are those more likely to cheat in an effort to achieve the highest possible score.

The only real and valid argument against cheating is that by doing so, you're indirectly negatively affecting other students who *didn't* cheat. This is true, and most students don't want to hurt others; they don't see their classmates as the enemy, it's the system that they're against. As a result, we see group cheating becoming the new norm. Tragically, comradery aids the authority at fishing out the culprits— friends help friends of friends, and somewhere in between, word gets out. As a second order consequence, the honest student who tips the teacher becomes 'the rat'. Suffice to say, this furthers social issues.

I, too, have cheated my fair share in school. It's really not that tough, especially with a team. A group of us used to collude routinely as we all could benefit. We knew that they might catch us individually, but together, we were unstoppable. This is not to say that the school didn't actively take measures to curb cheating. They were quite relentless— plagiarism detection software, several moderators scanning the room and even pat-downs before entering the exam hall. These measures may have slowed us, but they never could solve the problem. Looking back, the amount of effort we put into gaming the system is quite impressive. And that's precisely why they couldn't eradicate cheating! The system *could* be gamed—kids understand this earlier than people think—and the more control is enforced (instead of fixing the underlying issue) the more people will retaliate. If I knew truly how useless grades were in real life, I wouldn't have bothered to cheat. Which is why, during my four years of college, I haven't cheated once. I simply don't care about the grade. I see it for the sham it is. And now that I get to learn what I want to learn in my spare time, taking shortcuts is actually counterproductive.

In conclusion, today, cheating is a win-win-win. Students, parents and schools, even if they don't explicitly say it, all prefer to turn a blind-eye. Teachers benefit as they look better when their students get higher grades. And if they do start enforcing the rules and doling out punishments, parents are always ready to put up a fight against accusations attacking their little baby.

The implications of treating college as the holy grail of education doesn't end with mandatory schooling. It successfully restricts the one thing that would get us out of this mess—innovation. To be fair, it's caused more by society's acceptance of the model, rather than by the model itself. I'll explain by example.

There are a bunch of new organizations attempting to solve the drawbacks of traditional schooling. One such initiative is *Big Picture Learning*. The core philosophy here is that for effective learning to take place, the student must be at the centre of education. In other words, the student must dictate what they should explore, when it's time to try something new and so on. The student is now the subject, not the object. All in all, this is a step in the right direction. In fact, this has been so successful that a plethora of schools have adopted this globally.[9]

The issue lies when scaling up. Most schools that adopt Big Picture Learning's philosophy have been restricted to middle school and younger because as soon as curriculum that is not accepted by colleges is implemented in the latter stages of K-12, nobody wants to go there (even if it's objectively better for learning). Schools diagnose the problem correctly and adopt the innovative educational philosophy, but, to attract students for high school (and sustain a business) they must opt-in for mainstream curriculum as well. Now, not to say that today's mainstream curricula doesn't have merits, but they do suffer from one core issue—the artificial imposition of time. For a deeper understanding of the implications of this, see Chapter 16.

By being forced to adapt to business demands, schools hinder their chances of addressing the original problem. So we find ourselves in a catch-22—a school cannot improve without being publicly accepted, and to be publicly accepted, they need to adopt the status quo.

ഗ

Overall, K-12 education has become more like employee preparation. After all, it was meant to be exactly that at inception. By no means am I attempting to denigrate the employee. For many—assuming culture fit, self-discipline, and savvy money management—devoting their careers to a successful company can lead to profound fulfillment and financial freedom. Nonetheless, the philosophies emphasized in K-12 schooling are eerily similar to those best suited for a Kafkaesque career—obedience and risk-avoidance being the two major pillars.

In class, you're expected to sit down, be quiet and listen to a teacher talk, even if you have no intention of listening to what is being said. You must do as they say. Anything other than what's expected is *incorrect*. You've made a mistake, and must rectify your behaviour. If not, you will be punished. Nowadays, punishments aren't as explicit as physical beatings, but authority figures do impose their expectations. Some subtle, like an annoyed tone in the teacher's voice, and some more obvious, like suspensions and detentions. This may not sound that bad, but 12 years of this! Making small holes sporadically in a large ship will eventually cause it to sink.

What's incredibly ironic is that *mistakes* are the most robust learning mechanism we have. They are the natural teachers of life. When we make a mistake doing something we enjoy, we actively avoid repeating it in the self-motivated pursuit of achieving our goal. But, when we're punished for a mistake made doing something we didn't want to do in the first place, we tend to find the path of least resistance rather than fully invest ourselves in growing as individuals.

The best example of this is the USA. Many people recognize the inadequacies of American formal education—that is literally what this book's about—but still, new phenomena with global impact tend to come from here. Why? Because America's greatest asset is a culture that encourages behaviour with asymmetric risk profiles—ideas that have a high risk to reward ratio. In other words, they love making educated mistakes. Unlike most dialogue from mainstream media, this is what makes America great—a willingness and ability to perform a rational, unemotional, and unbiased form of trial and error.

Coming back to education, this *mistake and risk-avoidance = a good thing* mentality is one of the greatest fallacies engrained in all children as it's the exact opposite of what is needed when trying *anything* new. Especially now, when old solutions no longer seem to be working for our new problems. Instead, today, K-12 is not preparing kids for the future or to be competitive in the workforce, it's only preparing them for college admissions. This is no trivial matter. It is precisely these faulty philosophies that are ever present during our formative years that dictate our values, and thus, our actions. *When you're young and impressionable, things that seem true are your truths.*

The most unfortunate part is that everything I've outlined here is happening within the most lavish schools. Needless to say, the scope of inefficacy is much greater in the vast majority of mid to low-tier schools. However, it is important to note that in spite of the politics intertwined with education, increasing this or that budget won't help us break through the glass ceiling that our most well-endowed schools seem to be trapped under. This is precisely why I have avoided making any comments on such hurdles that the majority of K-12 face and have focused more on the conceptual defects of the system.

In sum, as a result of the deteriorating quality of K-12, kids are coming out of, arguably, the most influential period of their life with nothing to show for it. This is why we have a growing number of students in college who not only struggle with foundational topics, but also who have gone there to *figure out what to do.* The latter is not inherently a problem, but the fact that a robust argument can be made claiming that higher education (the next stage in this joke that we call an education system) is doing a worse job than its junior counterparts, makes it a huge problem. The next few chapters investigate this very argument.

10

Our Young Adult Years

Before we begin, brace yourself. This is probably the most complex and potentially controversial section so far. I have no intention of offending anyone, and I apologize if I inadvertently do. I only want for you, the reader, to maximize your chances of success—whatever your definition of it is—and I truly believe the information I present is critical towards achieving that goal.

To be clear, I'm *not* anti-education, anti-learning or anything of that sort. I've experienced first-hand the effectiveness of self-education and the ineffectiveness of traditional schooling. And, I concede, at their respective quintessential best, a good teacher takes the cake every single day. But, it's the incredible ubiquity of misinformation and misconceptions about higher education present in society that prompted me to write this book in the first place.

It is no secret that those who attain further degrees have a better chance at earning higher salaries—clearly higher education works. But, like any path in life, that doesn't mean it will work for everyone in the same way. The NBA clearly works—look at Lebron—does that mean everyone should join the NBA? No. Investment Banking clearly works—look at Wall Street—does that mean everyone should head there? No. The same applies to college. I'm not undermining education—that is no doubt key—but unfortunately, given the conditions that have arisen today, college works for far fewer than it should. This is my stance.

This does not mean that I plan on painting a biased picture of the situation, but it does mean I will emphasize the facts supporting my case. The reasons for this are simple: (1) I don't need to reiterate the several benefits of higher education; society and educational institutions have already done so in their wonderfully coy rhetoric. (2) The drawbacks of higher education tend to be overlooked in mainstream dialogue. Why? Because these marginalized arguments don't provide the incentive to be backed by millions of dollars; there is a huge time-lag until they become evident; they haven't been experienced by older generations; and most importantly, they tend to be misunderstood when we bring emotions into the conversation.

My goal is to provide the other side of the story such that readers may take into account all the relevant information, and then make an informed decision about their own path.

11

What is college?

The stereotypical four-year higher education institution primarily offers five value propositions:

1. **Liberal Arts Education/Core/General Education**
   Critical thinking, Ability to reason, Creative thinking, Connecting the dots, Questioning timeless truths, Communication, etc.
2. **Practical Skills/Real World Job-Skills**
   Computer Science, Marketing, Engineering, etc.
3. **Accreditation/The Degree**
   For which you must fulfil specific requirements. These include, but are not limited to:
   a. Completion of X credit hours. For each class, the student receives X number of credit hours.
      i. Completion of X credit hours of Lower Division classes.
      ii. Completion of X credit hours of Upper Division classes.
   b. Passing X number of Core/General-Ed classes.
   c. Passing X number of Major-specific classes.
   d. Passing X number of Elective classes.
   e. Attain a minimum of an X GPA.
4. **Networking**
   This includes opportunities to establish connections with alumni, to meet students of diverse backgrounds and abilities, to connect

with companies with existing ties to the university, etc.

5. **Self-Discovery/Figuring Out What You Like and Dislike**
   This includes opportunities to learn how to live independently, join clubs/communities of various purposes, try new activities, develop new interests, take classes from an almost endless array of topics (Electives), etc.

If someone asked me, 'Would you send your kid to a place like this?' I, too, would say yes in a heartbeat; especially considering the historical life outcomes of attending such institutions.

And what were said outcomes?

12

What was college?

Today, a college student needs to navigate a very different world than times before. The major difference being the road from education to employment. Back in the post-WWII environment, rapid technological advancement resulted in a massive shift among the drivers of the world economy. A pattern common to all of them was the need for highly specialized skills; a phenomenon that economists call *skill-biased technological change*. This greatly benefitted the college graduate; the great shortage in skilled labour caused by the sudden shift in the nature of work led to an explosion in their demand.

This made the education-to-work journey straightforward and predictable—excel in high school, get into the most reputed university possible, graduate and, subsequently, line up to meet employers. When a good fit is found, a person could safely expect a lifelong career at that company. Importantly, back then, the surplus of jobs available for graduates gave *all* the leverage to the degree holder.[1]

In 1948, Fortune magazine described the trend as:

Corporate men who work the college circuit for likely executive material—'ivory hunting' in the trade jargon—complain that the market has never been so unruly. Prices are up at least 100 percent over 1941, and students…are having a wonderful time playing hard to get.[2]

The next question naturally becomes, 'What was it that made a degree so valuable in the eyes of employers?' To understand that we must first understand what a degree exactly is.

The diploma, or any form of accreditation for that matter, is one and only one thing: a filtration mechanism. Its value is not derived from some inherent property of the piece of paper, but from the collective agreement of its value between us humans. It's like money, well kind of. In most countries, having national currency is far more valuable than owning any other currency. Why? Because it's what everybody uses! If nobody used it, it wouldn't be worth anything. Likewise, the pursuit to earn a degree became a worthy pursuit only because employers made it so.

See, those responsible for hiring faced a problem that pretty much everybody will at some point—constraints posed by limited resources. As urbanization and procreation did its thing, employers were receiving an increasing number of applicants from radically different backgrounds, and there was no efficient method to assess a complete stranger's potential to do the job, let alone ascertain if they're a good fit for the company's culture.

So, they were forced to look for signals that conveyed the most information with the least amount of resources, which just so happened to be done best by the college diploma.

Organizations are built around rules and expectations. To be considered a good employee, one must: show up at the expected time, act in adherence to the established rules, stay until the end of the day and, most importantly, do so over a sustained period of time. College degrees, then, become a pretty good indicator—why utilize precious time and money on assessing a candidate if college has already done it for you? It was nowhere near perfect, but certainly the best from the available options.

What made it so?

Officially, a degree certifies the completion of a course of study. But that's the last thing employers care about. In reality, the diploma conveys a lot more; albeit, it's highly dependent on the source. For example, those from elite colleges signal a high level of cognitive ability—not because of some special knowledge received there, but because they were accepted into it in the first place. Kevin Carey said it best:

> 'Harvard dropout' and 'Harvard graduate' are almost identical in what they say about a person.[3]

However, in a time where the world's knowledge was, for the most part, concentrated in large institutions known as universities, a degree also signalled that the candidate has had exposure to content, modes of thinking, etc. that were simply unattainable elsewhere; in the pre-internet days, colleges had a monopoly on sophisticated knowledge. More importantly, a degree proves the completion of a lengthy process filled with instruction and responsibility. For four years, one must independently register for classes, show up on time, complete assignments and pass examinations.

For these reasons, employers found the diploma to be an efficient and robust mechanism for talent identification. Economists call this *statistical discrimination*—the use of true-on-average observations to save resources.[4] Even though the claim that this is unfair may not be completely false, this phenomenon is present in many walks of life. For example, senior citizens tend to pay a higher premium on life insurance because they tend to die sooner. Humans are wired to be attracted to good physique because they tend to produce healthier offspring. We avoid restaurants with negative reviews because they are more likely to serve bad food. We ignore get-rich-quick advertisements because they tend to be scams.

For the student, this meant that college was almost always a timely positive return on investment. The ratio of degree holders to well-paying employment opportunities was extremely lopsided. It was a no-brainer for employers to snatch up every available graduate. Moreover, during this time, the cost of attending institutes of higher education was not a financial burden. One could work a summer job or even a minimum-wage job through the school year (without sacrificing academics) to pay for tuition. Today, the same would be like trying to empty an ocean with a bucket. Undoubtedly, the facilities, diversity of student population, alumni pool and other such factors are much more comprehensive today, but the cost has risen far beyond a student's means to afford it.

This statement should *not* be taken lightly. The financial reality that comes with the path a person takes in their education must be the top priority. It may be accompanied by other factors, but it must be second to none. This is because our lives are governed by our financial realities. Think about it, please, especially if you haven't yet.

Almost every action one takes is in some way or form an income for another. Have a bed? Income for the manufacturer. Leases a house? Income for the landlord. Playing video games? Income for the video-game creator, TV manufacturer, electricity provider and internet provider. Drive a car? Income for the car manufacturer and gas/electricity company. On social media? Income for the platform, every second, especially if you end up making a purchase.

The goal, obviously, is to minimize expenses while maximizing income. And the issue is everyone pretends to understand this concept, but very few display this understanding in their behaviour.

$100 for healthy groceries? Too expensive.

$100 for dinner at a nice restaurant? Reasonable.

$200 for a networking seminar? Not worth it.

$200 for a weekend drinking? Weekly occurrence.

$500 for an online course? Rip off.

$500 for designer clothes? Got to have it.

$1000 to invest? Too risky.

$1000 for the new iPhone? You get my point.

I'll say it again, future financial realities should never be taken lightly. For many, however, a large number of financial decisions come at the expense of their future selves. But do you know what is expensive? Taxes, raising a family, mortgage payments... *life* is expensive. I'm not undermining the value of spontaneity; some of the best memories in life are unplanned. I'm just trying to say that, based on the evidence, our priorities are wack.

We, as a generation (talking to the millennials and younger here), have a very irrational sense of optimism. Now, we shouldn't be pessimists; having a positive outlook towards life is a good thing, but the idea that *everything will work out* is deeply entrenched in our psyche. Can you blame us? We haven't lived through any *real sh*t*! Don't get me wrong, 2008 was bad, Covid-19 caught everyone off-guard, and there are plenty of appalling conflicts taking place all over the world. But, to say that those could even compare to two of the most brutal wars in all of human history *and* the fact that we were on the brink of nuclear Armageddon (and that's in the last century alone!), is extremely arrogant. Just for a second, transport yourself back in time. Can you imagine how your life would've been? If you can't form a vivid picture for yourself, the following should give you a pretty good idea.

Let's say you were born at the turn of the last century. It's the early 1900s, technology is exploding; the telephone, the car and electricity are going mainstream. The world's full of optimism, and then, suddenly... for your eighteenth birthday, here's WWI—the Great War. Four years of absolute hell, and just as the sh*t-show comes to an end... the Spanish Flu. The virus killed more people than the goddamn war! Okay, you survived both events. Surely things will get better now, right? Nope. The Great Depression. The Rise of Fascism. Oh, you thought WWI was the war to end all wars? The last one? Here's WWII, with a side of holocaust. Okay, you've somehow managed to pass your fiftieth birthday in one piece—you absolute legend! Now, at least, you can live your twilight years in peace. Sorry, Mr Khrushchev has other ideas. Enter the Cold War. The world is literally on the verge of nuclear annihilation. To give you an idea, here's Steve Jobs, arguably one of the most focused and driven minds that has graced this planet, on life during the Cold War.

> I probably didn't sleep for three or four nights because I was afraid that if I went to sleep, I wouldn't wake up.[5]

And that, my friend, would have been life in the 20th century. I don't think any of us can comprehend emotions such as these without actually experiencing them—but learn, we must, from the past.

Anyway, let's get back to the point. Higher education has never been this expensive! I'll let the numbers do the talking for me.

∽

- From 1980 to 2010, tuition has increased at more than double the rate of home prices, and the Consumer Price Index.[6]
- College tuition and fees see 1,120 per cent increase between 1978 to 2012.[7]
- From 1989 to 2016, the cost of college increased almost eight times quicker than wages.[8]
- From 1983 to 2014, discounting for inflation, the real cost of tuition and other fees have increased 250 per cent in private colleges and 330 per cent in public colleges. During the same time, real wages remained relatively constant.[9]
- As you can see, even though the numbers differ from source to source, the general trend is clear: the cost of college is moving unsustainably upward.

13

Why is college so expensive?

Well…it's complicated. There are several reasons why the cost of higher education is where it is today. Let's break them down individually.

Perceived Value and Status Symbols

Humans are very weird creatures. And one reason that makes us so, is the love for earning a higher social status *and* the need to make it known to others. You see, we've always organized ourselves in hierarchies, in fact, almost all social mammals do. We're not sure what part of the brain corresponds to this observation, but we see children as young as fifteen-months *infer social ranking based on their own experiences.*[1]

Why is this relevant?

Well, as the explosion in demand for higher education was met with an increasing amount of supply, the need for a mechanism to help students make an informed decision arose. Consequently, we got the first-ever college rankings. Gradually, because of our tendency to attain a higher status, students began to behave like consumers, spending months (if not years) identifying the best deal in the market. Thus, an evolution occurred in what it means to be a successful college. A superior college wasn't one that was objectively better for learning, it was one that was perceived to be superior by the public! Suffice to say, college rankings embody this perception.

∽

The *US News and World Report*, arguably the most sought-after college ranking, published their inaugural list in 1983. Back when information was sparse, it solved a real problem. Now, information is everywhere. You can learn about a college by contacting (theoretically) any student, professor and/or faculty member via the internet. Still, colleges actively work towards climbing up these rankings; an endeavour that demands capital akin to the first world's demand for energy.

Hence, the vicious cycle continues to spin.

The higher their rank, the more students apply, the more potential tuition revenue, the more resources can be allocated to climb further up.

The issue is, these rankings have become dangerously overrated. Coming back to *US News and World Report*, they state that their ranking methodology (for the year 2020) is as follows:[2]

Graduation and Retention Rates

Average. 6-year Graduation Rate	17.6%
Average 1st Year Retention Rate	4.4%

Social Mobility

PELL Grants Graduation Rates	2.5%
PELL Grants Graduation Rate Performance	2.5%

Graduation Rate Performance	8%
Undergraduate Academic Reputation by Peer Assessment Survey	20%

Faculty Resources

Class Size Index	8%
Faculty Compensation	7%
% of Faculty with a terminal degree in their respective field	3%

% of Faculty that is full-time	1%
Student-Faculty Ratio	1%
Student Selectivity	
SAT/ACT Scores	7.75%
Top 10% High School Standing	2.25%
Financial Resource per Student	10%
Average Alumni Giving Rate	5%

First, can we please acknowledge the arbitrariness of these criteria? No doubt, graduating from college is an integral part of the ride, but what makes it 17.6 per cent of the complete value proposition? Also, why have we normalized the six-year period to track graduation?! I thought it was supposed to be a four-year deal.

Next, 'Graduation Rate Performance' is defined as 'each college's actual six-year graduation rate with what we predicted for its fall 2012 entering class'. So, at the end of the day, almost a tenth of the ranking criteria is based on a prediction? And why 8 per cent? Considering graduation rates have already been given 17.6 per cent, that's quite a lot. Notice: more than a quarter of the ranking is derived from the act of graduation, and not once are real student learning outcomes considered.

I'm in disbelief, but this is nowhere close to the end.

20 per cent for a survey? They call it 'Expert Opinion' and define it as a 'measure of how a school is regarded by administrators at peer institutions on a peer assessment survey'. Obviously, the butcher is going to say the meat is fresh, and apparently, an opinion from within the industry is worth a juicy 20 per cent.

Moving on, 'Class Size Index' at 8 per cent. They define it as a measure to assess 'the ability of students to engage with their instructors in class. Schools receive the most credit in this index for their proportions of undergraduate classes with fewer than twenty students. Classes with 20 to 29 students score second-highest, 30 to 39 students third highest and 40 to 49 students fourth highest. Classes that are 50 or more students receive no credit'. How in the world can class size alone measure how engaged students are? Student engagement is a product of several factors: the professor's knowledge, the professor's ability to teach, student's attendance in class, student's willingness to learn, etc. I, along with many others, have all too often found myself in small classes that were deplorably unengaging, while classes two-to-three times the size being anything but. To say student engagement can be measured with their definition is exactly like saying IQ alone is a robust measure of life success. It is a blatant attempt to deceive while being perceived as intellectual.

I'm going to save these rankings from any further embarrassment.

However, there is one thing that *needs* to be understood. Regardless of the ranking rationale offered, under all the jargon lies a single important factor—how much money is the college investing in itself. It is money that enables the availability of scholarships to attract students with higher academic scores. It is money that attracts better professors looking for higher pay in the private sector or at schools with stronger financials. It is money that creates and maintains the state-of-the-art facilities that persuade students to pick college X over college Y (often, these facilities have no effect on learning outcomes). And it is money that builds each of the student-support systems that are deemed necessities today.

Do not be deceived by the *non-profit* tag; a college's primary objective may not be to make a profit, but it's well in their interest to maximize revenue to plow back into expansion. While I acknowledge that some colleges are better than others, we don't need rankings to know that. In other words, yearly rankings for colleges are like quarterly financial reports for public companies. Sure, they provide some idea about the institution, but it heavily incentivizes short-term, artificial progress at the expense of long-term, real growth.

All this being said, the problem isn't one-sided. The fact that rankings exist does not make their creators or the institutes using them propagators of evil. It is the consumers—us—our reaction to these rankings that has allowed the negative side-effects to manifest. As a humble request, I ask everybody—students, parents, teachers, politicians and everybody in between—please consider the ranking methodology before giving it a value it doesn't deserve.

∽

Of course, the Ivies and the rest of the old guard withstood this evolution in higher education unscathed, courtesy of their reputation and history. However, with only the top spots occupied, fierce competition raged for the next highest digits. So, the question beckons: what would make a college be perceived as superior?

Objectively speaking, there is no argument against the fact that learning outcomes should play a major role in determining such a status. But this metric, however, has one key drawback—the ability to convey this information. After all, what good is status if no one knows about it? It can take incredible amounts of resources for a college to achieve a high-perceived value by improving learning outcomes; as all the signals depend on alumni and hence have a huge time-lag to be visible. And, as we've already established, colleges need a higher perceived value *now*. The next rankings will be published in less than twelve months! So, instead, colleges look to designer brands for inspiration.

Let's do a quick thought experiment, and be honest.

Think about that one item from a designer brand that you would buy if the opportunity arises. Now, let's make it available at every outlet mall and make the price identical to its non-luxury alternatives. Would you still have the same strong urge to make the purchase? For most, I predict the answer will be no. This is because their value is derived from scarcity and price. The limited availability and high price-tag are the product, not attributes of the product. And they're both extremely visible—just Google it.

Scarcity is pretty straightforward. The less percentage of applicants that get in, the greater the achievement. Naturally then, if someone attended a school with a 5 per cent (as opposed to a 35 per cent) acceptance rate, they would be held in higher regard. There is no inherent malice here, especially if a college gets many more applicants than its capacity, but this is worth noting as it is used to justify tuition hikes.

As for artificial price increase, it's not as straightforward as it is for designer brands. If a college simply tripled its price with no difference in offerings, a simple college visit would bring their ambitions crumbling down. But what if they incrementally increase tuition which, when combined with debt, can finance massive infrastructural projects? And this is exactly what is happening. Visit any college campus! On most, there will definitely be some major construction project scheduled to start in the near future, one that is going on now, and/or one that was recently completed. The whole trend can be aptly described as the *Higher Education Arms Race*. The cost of which is promptly passed on to students.

We could go back and forth on why almost every department needs their own classrooms—as if a management and a psychology course have different classroom requirements—but let's not get into that argument. Instead, I ask, did the college really need that rock-climbing wall? Did it need the housing structure that could be mistaken for a five-star hotel? Did the library really need a renovation? Hell, in some schools, they also have several music festivals annually! And that's not all. Schools pour millions of dollars into college athletics. Coaches are paid seven-figure salaries, grandiose facilities are built and generous scholarships are used to recruit players. All to further the college's athletic status in the national pool—whether it is American football, basketball, volleyball or any other sport. Worst of all, these expenses are rarely recouped; they're almost always a net-negative to the school's financials. And again, the burden of which is usually passed on to the average student.[3] I'm not against college athletics by any means; in fact, I'm a huge advocate of sports. What I am against, however, is using athletics as a marketing tool, especially in colleges where the vast majority of students are not there to become athletes.

At the end of the day, it is the regular student who is financing the gimmick of non-academic related facilities, which he will never use (okay, maybe once).

∽

The following is a real-life case study that demonstrates what has been presented thus far:

Stephen Joel Trachtenberg became president of George Washington (GW) University in 1988. In spite of having no access to capital via the government or rich alumni, he was told, 'Make this place better… and by the way, be embarrassed that you're not Georgetown.'[4] At the time, the university had a relatively obscure reputation, but he knew that higher education was now in the luxury market. Colleges were selling a signal of success—a rite of passage to a higher-class— not education. Aware of the principals of perceived value (price and scarcity), his plan was simple: Fake it till you make it. He would convince people of the university's value by charging more money. Don't believe me? Kevin Carey, the director of the Education Policy Program at New America, interviewed Trachtenberg on the subject. Here's what he had to say.

> College is like vodka…Vodka is by definition a flavourless beverage. It all tastes the same. But people will spend $30 for a bottle of Absolut vodka because of the brand. A Timex watch costs $20, a Rolex $10,000. They both tell the same time. An expensive degree serves as a trophy, a symbol…For the buyer, it's a sort of token of who they think they are.[5]

The plan worked. When he came to power in 1988, tuition was around \$9,500.[6] When he left in 2007, it cost \$37,000—one of the most expensive in the entire country.[7] In the same time-span, the number of applicants significantly rose, providing the cash flow to build grandiose facilities. At one point, only seven colleges in America—all Ivy Leagues—had a varsity squash program for men and women. Guess who started the eighth?

GW was not alone in this. Competition for the tuition dollars was nationwide. As Trachtenberg said:

> We built a new building, they built two new buildings. It was like those gangster movies where they say, 'You kill one of my guys, I kill two of your guys.' That's what was going on all the time.[8]

Carey's reflection of his conversation with Trachtenberg continued:

> I asked Trachtenberg if it was morally defensible to let students borrow tens of thousands of dollars for a service that he himself had compared to a valueless luxury good…'I'm not embarrassed by what we did,' he said. 'It's not as if it's some kind of a bait and switch here. It's not as if the faculty weren't good. It's not as if the opportunities to get a good degree weren't there. There's no misrepresentation here.' When I noted that some other college had recently passed GW in having the highest price, he said that wouldn't have happened on his watch. He would have kept it going.[9]

☙

Over time, as tuition rises to rates like those today, it all seems worth it, at least from an outsider's point of view. We assume a higher cost means better quality education, which helps us rationalize the expense—naively. I find it all incredibly ironic: potential students come for a campus visit, an *existing* student sells them on the great facilities, but neither will we ever hear about the financial burden the student tour guide is under right now, nor about the same burden the potential student will be under in due time. Not once will the state-of-the-art recreation centres come to their rescue.

I confess, it's all very convincing. After all, I was sold the same narrative and bought it. The physical shiny-new exterior only pushes the student who has no idea what he wants in life towards the maw of the tuition bill.

Non-Teaching Staff

So, we have all these mega-recreational centres, multi-storied luxury dormitories, well-endowed athletic departments and overall pristine campus'. It's paid for, it's built, but now it has to be maintained.

Due to the single-minded goal of expansion, every new project—athletic programs, infrastructure, cultural offices, etc.—adds to the school's fixed costs. From which, a fraction of the financial burden is inevitably passed on to the student. And just to be clear, it's a lot! I was dumbfounded when I found out about the sheer number of administrative staff schools employ relative to teaching faculty.

∽

- From 1993 to 2007:[10]
    - Full-time administrators per 100 American universities grew by 39 per cent
    - Teaching staff per 100 American universities grew by only 18 per cent
    - Inflation-adjusted administrative spending per student increased 61 per cent
- From 1975 to 2011, full-time non-faculty professionals at universities increased by 369 per cent.[11]

∽

Former president of the University of California system, Clark Kerr, called this the *multiversity system*.[12] He foresaw the increase in administrative faculty, each with their own department, pursuing their own discrete goal—from marketing to fundraising to legal compliance—to inevitably fuel more of the same.[13] He was correct.[14] In fact, not only has the size of administration bloated, but also has its responsibilities.[15] The net result of which is student learning to tumble down the list of priorities.[16]

With expenses rising, colleges must look to other areas for cost-savings. Ironically, one of these areas is teaching staff! Colleges, *whose primary responsibility is to teach*, are proactively hiring adjunct professors—who earn as little as $3,000 per course[17]—to teach every additional course the school may add to their catalogue. It's borderline humorous to see how they've gotten away by hiding in plain sight; institutions constantly boast about the variety of courses offered, but we never seem to question their ability to actually teach it.

Bringing me to my next point.

Unnecessary Class Offerings

At the bare minimum, every class needs a teacher and a place to be conducted—both expenses that rack up quickly. And the number of different classes offered by colleges, especially in the USA, can very easily be in the several hundred, if not thousands. A majority of which any single student will not even hear about, let alone consider taking.

I get it, 'Electives', the diverse assortment of classes offered by schools is what allows one to taste different fields of study, which may lead to invaluable self-discovery of likes, dislikes, capacities, etc. But there is a lot ignored from this rationale—namely the *Upper-Division Elective*.

College is a four-year trip. We're told that for the first two years, we have the opportunity to try whatever we want, we're not bound by anything. So, if we complete all our experimenting by year-two, why is it mandatory to take Electives in year-three and four? If we've declared what we want to pursue, shouldn't we only focus on that for the time we have remaining?

I wholeheartedly acknowledge that the majority (or at least a significant minority), may not have their path in life figured out by the two-year mark. There is nothing wrong with that. But the argument to propagate mandatory electives throughout one's time in college is as robust as an ice cube in a fire. This is so for two reasons. (1) Doesn't such a policy undermine the value of the initial selling point of electives? If it's not fulfilling its purpose in the time it's meant to, maybe we're missing something. (2) By now, it's practically impossible for a student to change their course of study without incurring significant costs. One reason for this is prerequisites. I hold no objection against taking courses sequentially, but the need to take a specific set of lower-division classes *before* being able to access the upper-division classes results in additional monetary and temporal costs for those who desire to switch fields of study in year three or four.

Point is, if such factors and implications exist, shouldn't it be optional for one to take these classes during our last two years? In marketing, there is a term for this—the upsell. When successful, the system comes with a whole host of hidden expenses that eerily mirror a sleazy salesman trying to sell existing customers on yet *another* product. In this case, another year or two of school.

Upper Division electives—alongside the plethora of academic programs with low-demand and high unemployment rates—are an unnecessary and significant cost for many students. Unfortunately, the provision of classes geared for only a few students that end up being paid for by all doesn't end there.

In recent times, there has been an explosion in remedial class offerings in institutions of higher education. Ignoring the oxymoronic nature of that statement, this, too, significantly drives up the costs incurred by the student.

cs

- A 2006 study found about 40 per cent of traditional undergraduates took at least one remedial course.[18]
- In 2008, 1 in 5 first-year students in American degree-granting institutes were taking remedial classes covering high-school material.[19]

cs

There's no *explicit* reason for this, but we can make the following inferences:

1. Colleges have decided to re-educate students out of their own love for education.

   Or,

2. Students enrolling in college need to be re-educated.

If the former is true, then I request that enrollment into these classes be made optional, such that the cost burden doesn't fall onto *every single* student. Assuming one has a solid foundation in high school material, the entire first year of college is like high school *on repeat*. Why are we paying upwards of $20,000 dollars for yet another year of high school in shiny-new repackaging? If the latter is true, then it says a lot about the college admission process. Why are more and more kids being admitted when they are not ready for the material? I certainly don't mean this in an elitist manner, but doesn't this undermine the whole concept of a *higher* education? It would be much more cost-effective for all parties involved if students just took a year to brush up on foundational material and then applied to colleges, especially considering the availability of free online resources.

Budget Cuts

This is pretty straightforward. In a nutshell, as subsidies from the government are reduced, institutes compensate for the reduction in revenue by increasing the cost burden on the student—especially in public schools where tuition was already at the lowest rate due to government aid.[20] When we couple all the aforementioned growing costs for the college with a reduction in government subsidies, it is no surprise that we get skyrocketing tuition fees.

∽

- In 2017, the average US state spent sixteen per cent less per student than in 2008. In other words, higher education funding has been scaled back by $9 billion.[21]

∽

But hold on, just because something is expensive does not mean that it isn't worth it. Even if the above statement may be true, for the most part, college isn't worth it.

Here's why.

14

So…how did we get here?

First and foremost, let me address what exactly I mean by *here*. Obviously, when compared to a century ago, our species is in a much better position right now, and it would be incredibly unfair to not acknowledge the education system's role in achieving this feat. However, hopefully, it is also equally obvious that there is a lot wrong within those same institutions. Still, the *go-to-college* narrative marches on with steadfast resilience. With this in mind, *here* can be best described by three observations that have manifested in higher education: tuition hikes, ideological inbreeding and unsustainable student debt.

Skyrocketing Tuition

For a refresher, read the preceding chapter.

Ideological Inbreeding

This point alone is deserving of an entire book, in fact, it got one—*The Coddling of the American Mind,* by Greg Lukianoff and Jonathan Haidt. Hence, for the sake of brevity, I will simplify.

Essentially, colleges are facilitating the growth of very harmful modes of thought amongst students and, thus, society. They are doing so not by explicitly advocating for said modes, but by turning a blind eye to them. To provide some clarity, I will introduce a phenomenon that has manifested on the college campus. One that I believe *is*, and will continue to be, crippling for the individual more than anything. It is the censorship of ideas and information predicated on the emotional response it evokes. Students are demanding protection from points of view that have scope to offend or create discomfort.

∽

- In a 2017 survey, 58 per cent of students said, 'It is important to be part of a campus community where I am not exposed to intolerant and offensive ideas.'[1]

∽

Colleges are feeding into this doctrine in four major ways.

1. **The removal of course material**. For example: in Columbia University's General Education Core Curriculum, there is a course titled *Masterpieces of Western Literature and Philosophy*. By design, it is meant to tackle 'the most difficult questions about human experience.'[2] Surprisingly, in a 2015 school newspaper article, to substantiate the claim that 'Students need to feel safe in the classroom,' a small group of undergraduates wrote that many texts in the Western canon are, 'wrought with histories and narratives of exclusion and oppression' and contain 'triggering and offensive material that marginalizes student identities in the classroom.'[3] I bring this up not to undermine these students and their argument, but to revisit a very integral principle in the quest for wisdom. Considering there is no tangible danger present, is it wise to prioritize discomfort and emotional angst over knowledge?

2. Censorship occurs due to the fear of being demonized for individual views. In other words, **the rise of call-out culture**, where individuals are lionized for publicly pointing out small (often trivial) offenses

committed by someone else. This has become yet another barrier in the free exchange of ideas throughout the university system, especially with the amplifying power of social media. Best described as walking on eggshells, students are afraid to say something that might be considered offensive, or even defend someone else out of fear of being mobbed on social media.[4]

One college student had this to say:

During my first days at [college], I witnessed countless conversations that consisted of one person telling the other that their opinion was wrong. The word 'offensive' was almost always included in the reasoning. Within a few short weeks, members of my freshman class had quickly assimilated to this new way of non-thinking. They could soon detect a politically incorrect view and call the person out on their 'mistake'. I began to voice my opinion less often to avoid being berated and judged by a community that claims to represent the free expression of ideas.[5]

Another said,

I probably hold back 90 per cent of the things that I want to say due to fear of being called out…People won't call you out because your opinion is wrong. People will call you out for literally anything. On Twitter today, I came across someone making fun of a girl who made a video talking about how much she loved God and how she was praying for everyone. There were hundreds of comments, rude comments, below the video. It was to the point that they weren't even making fun of what she was standing for. They were picking apart everything. Her eyebrows, the way her mouth moves, her voice, the way her hair was parted. Ridiculous.[6]

The rise of 'call-out culture'

This, unfortunately, isn't only a student-side issue. A large number of the professoriate, too, are increasingly cautious about what they say and the words they use.[7] The trend of being attacked for mere misunderstandings has spared no one.

3. **Skewed exposure to political views**. Note: the last thing I want is to veer into politics. Nonetheless, this is important to consider when trying to understand how our universities are slipping onto pathways that promote anti-intellectual thought process. Today, the ratio of left-leaning professors to right-leaning ones at universities stands around 5:1.[8] However, the numbers are even more telling when we consider the same ratio in the liberal arts departments. For example, in academic psychology, the ratio, from the mid-1990s to 2016, skyrocketed from 4:1 to 17:1.[9] In fact, the ratios in many of the central fields within the humanities are almost all above 10:1.[10]

Moreover, the problem of imbalanced exposure to points of view has clearly manifested itself through not only highly controversial events, such as Bill C-16 in Canada, but also a general shift to the left in younger generations. Now, there is neither anything inherently wrong with left-leaning ideologies, nor with its antithesis. However, the dangers posed on the extremes of both are very real and detrimental to all. The point is that today's students are more than well-acquainted with how right-wing extremism manifests itself; WWII and the Nazis are present in all stages of the education system in some shape or form. Comparatively, sources to gain exposure to either the calamities and eventual capitulation of the USSR/Mao's China, or the pitfalls of left-wing ideology are elusive, to say the least.

4. **Guest speaker disinvitation**. Disguised as claims for safety, the argument that the contents of a guest speaker's message may offend some students or cause discomfort, is often used to *cancel* talks. When these demands aren't met with swift acceptance, students threaten coordinated, loud and disruptive protests, effectively disallowing any

discourse from taking place.[11] Take UC Berkeley. In 2017, the campus witnessed extremely violent protests to prevent a guest speaker. Fires erupted, windows were broken, bystanders were pepper-sprayed and even Molotov cocktails found their way onto the scene.[12] Property damage exceeded half-a-million-dollars.[13] End result: the talk canceled and none of the student-perpetrators punished.

Intriguingly, it was on the very same campus that student, Mario Savio, led the campus free speech movement in 1964.[14] He preached the power of peaceful protest and the importance of freedom in speech. Less than a century later, the students of Berkeley seemed to ignore the irony.

A similar incident took place at Claremont McKenna College when Heather Mac Donald was scheduled to speak on her theories of the unintended side-effects caused by social activism. Essentially, she warned about how the *Black Lives Matter* movement could lead to increased crime in certain neighborhoods.[15] Instead, students saw her views as racist and decided to block the lecture-hall's entrance. She was ultimately forced to evacuate through a backdoor and into a police vehicle due to the dangerous disruption.[16]

These aren't just cherry-picked events. The Foundation for Individual Rights in Education has been tracking such incidents since 2000. According to their database, a whole 46 per cent of the disinvitation attempts since then have been successful, and about a third of the events that did proceed were disrupted by protesters to some degree.[17]

The key takeaway here is that the number of disinvitations is on the rise. With that, the idea that the very presence of a speaker equates danger.

∽

The following graph depicts disinvitation attempts each year since 2000.[18]

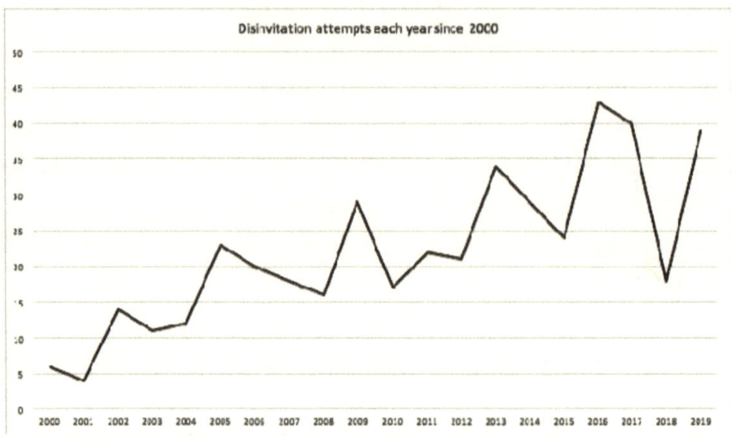

By playing into the conclusions put forward by emotional group-thinking, the universities themselves endorse the point of view that, in education, comfort is primary, truth secondary. Of course, the fallacious nature of this belief depends on your definition of education. Based on what I put forward earlier, this line of reasoning is deeply flawed. The argument that a lecture should be canceled because a student may be offended holds woefully little water. They conveniently ignore the fact that a demand to curb offense may very well be offensive to another, leading us into a circular path where nothing of substance is discussed or accomplished.

The reality is that things that are important to talk about are precisely topics that reside closest to the heart, and inherently come with a large probability of causing offense. It is better for all if we align our actions as per the words of Hanna Holborn Gray, the president of the University of Chicago from 1978 to 1993: 'Education should not be intended to make people comfortable; it is meant to make them think.'[19] And, as Dr Peterson said, 'In order to be able to think, you have to risk being offensive.'[20]

Hanna Holborn Gray

'Education should not be intended to make people comfortable;
it is meant to make them think.'

The punchline for all should be as follows: truth does not care about your brain's limbic response. Don't change your truth based on how you feel. Learn and grow from how you feel based on truth. Further, the world does not exist in binary systems; things are not *always* either good *or* bad.

Ignorance of these concepts are symptoms of ideological inbreeding. And increasingly, people throughout society are displaying them. Citizens of all ages are now only satisfied when the world is presented in black and white. As soon as they don't understand something, the notion that the situation is being intentionally obfuscated floods their perception.

But it isn't!

The world isn't black and white. All identity is intertwined. The moon is only bright because it reflects the sunshine.[21]

Never must we forget the learnings of Aleksandr Solzhenitsyn; the man experienced what the massacre of millions looks like! He teaches us about the fickle nature of our subjective views that determines what is right and wrong, how deceivingly convenient it is, and most importantly, how destructive it can be. Take this to your heart, my friend:

> If only it were so simple! If only there were evil people somewhere insidiously committing evil deeds, and it were necessary only to separate them from the rest of us and destroy them. But the line dividing good and evil cuts through the heart of every human being.[22]

For the individual, by no means does this imply that making sense of everything is an easy endeavour. It takes energy, time, focus and renunciation of the ego. Unfortunately, this is not what colleges are teaching students. Instead, by giving in to the demands of inexperienced minds, they implicitly convey that attaining a sound and nuanced understanding of an issue, *before trying to fix it,* is not necessary. I am not saying that the vast majority of protests are unfounded. I am only saying that it is dangerous when mass groupthink leads many to naively disregard the inadequacies in their own understanding of the very issue they aspire to solve. And when one points this out, we go back to square one—the conclusion that *the other* is trying to pull a fast one.

Bottom line: when schools don't explicitly take a stance against these dangerous doctrines, students inevitably fall victim to ideological inbreeding since diversity in opinion is increasingly non-existent. Much like how too much of the same genetic information results in deformed offspring in the biological world, too much bias is plaguing the world of knowledge. This is not to be taken lightly. Columbia University. Claremont Mackenna. UC Berkeley. These are arguably in the top one per cent of learning institutes worldwide. And they represent only the tip of the iceberg.

Student Debt

It is true. Mediocre learning outcomes and other such phenomena are difficult to quantify and measure. Debt, however, is easy to quantify. As of 4:37 p.m. on November 23, 2019, this is the amount of student debt in the USA (see live figure at *usdebtclock.org*):

$1,674,892,440,909

A trillion and a half symptoms of the disease that has plagued higher education! That last statement says a lot, but its gravity is often lost in communication due to our inability to understand large numbers. Can you conceptualize a trillion dollars? Most can't. It's tough, I know, but let me try.

How much time in days, months, years do you think represents a million seconds? Don't cheat. Take a stab at it.

11.5 days.

Now, try the same for a trillion seconds.

31,710 YEARS!

Clearly, one-trillion is an extremely large number. One-million is pocket change compared to it. Which makes the student debt crisis that much larger a problem. That said, I will let some cold hard facts do the talking.

၆

- As of 2019, student debt has eclipsed credit card debt and is second only to mortgage debt.
- For the first time in its history, The House Financial Services Committee held a hearing to discuss the student loan crisis.[23]
- From 1992 to 2014, the proportion of students with loans rose from 45 per cent to 71 per cent. In the same period, average debt increased from $9,000 to around $30,000.[24]
- By 2015, the average graduate owed $30,100 each.[25]
- 1 in 5 US households make student debt payments.[26]
- More than forty-million Americans owe student debt. 5.2 million are in delinquency to some degree. Every twenty-eight seconds a loan goes into default.[27]
- According to the New York Federal Reserve Bank, in 2012, the percentage of student loan balances 90+ days delinquent eclipsed the same for credit card loans.[28]

၆

I could not have said it better than the chief economist at the credit-rating behemoth, Moody's.

> We are creating a zombie generation of young people, landed with debt, and in many cases, dropouts without any diploma.[29]

And here's the kicker, this 'zombie generation' doesn't mean bad news only for the youth. Yes, they won't be able to afford a car or a down payment on a home, but in turn, the economy—i.e. everybody—will suffer death by a thousand cuts (or at least significant stagnation).[30]

Moving on. To understand how we've found ourselves in this unfortunate period in the history of higher education, we must first have a rudimentary understanding of complex systems. Not many of us are aware of complex systems—those composed of autonomous agents that produce emergent phenomena. In other words, a system that differs in characteristics from that of the individual parts that make the whole. These are present everywhere: the stock market, the human brain, ant colonies, the political landscape, cities and flocks of birds, to name a few. It's shocking that we aren't taught this in school, despite the fact that it embodies one of the most fundamental properties of our universe.

Consequently, at times, given the numerous components involved, what I'm saying might sound unnecessarily complicated. But it's precisely the existence of all these factors, simultaneously interacting in their own unique way, that has led to issues in the educational system. Neither, the cause of the problem nor any proposed solution, can be straightforward. To believe so is naive. Therefore, we must be willing to immerse ourselves in topics we're unfamiliar with if understanding is to be in the realm of possibility; especially when some of the topics—education, for example—are extremely important and often life-altering. So, with that, as promised at the beginning of the chapter, let's steam into how we have gotten here.

Institutional Isomorphism

This term was introduced by Paul DiMaggio and Walter Powel, a pair of Yale sociologists. Essentially, it describes the tendency of organizations within any given field to morph into one another over time.[31] In other words, it means that higher education institutes are copycats. Monkey see, monkey do—and the resulting effects have been monumental.

The first instance of isomorphism is the four-year model. Have you asked yourself why college takes four years to complete? Colleges don't—why question four years of revenue?

It began all the way back in the United Kingdom, before higher education was a thing in the United States. Henry Dunster, the first president of Harvard, picked up the four-year model from The University of Cambridge and put it into effect during the spring of 1652. A few years later, Cambridge switched to the three-year system, which as we know, is the standard today amongst many European colleges. And it just so happened that Dunster was *only* hired because his predecessor, Nathaniel Eaton, was accused of beating students. If he had carried on for just a few more years, we could've very well seen the proliferation of the three-year system in the USA as well—saving students' time and millions of tuition dollars in the process.[32]

Another phenomenon that nobody questions is the use of the credit hour as a measure of learning. After all, it is a requirement set in stone to earn a degree. It easily is overlooked just because everyone else follows the same requirements. But, there's nothing inevitable or ideal about it. Back in the early 1900s, many professors were paid poorly, so the industrialist, Andrew Carnegie, decided to create a fund (modern-day *TIAA-CREF*) to provide a free pension for full-time professors. Naturally, that required a definition of '*full-time*', for which they came up with the credit-hour. To qualify, a professor must hit twelve-credit-hours (four courses that meet three-hours per week for fifteen-weeks). Clearly, the credit-hour was never made to be used as a measure for student learning! Colleges knew this but used it anyway, as it provided a convenient and illusory mechanism to quantify learning of the vastly disjointed class offerings.

Moreover, we can trace the entire design of college as we know it to isomorphic roots. In the post-civil-war-era, higher education didn't have a formal structure. It focused predominantly on the various facets of ancient western civilization, and being exclusive to the elite class, felt little pressure to change. Soon, the idea of higher-education as a growth opportunity for *all*, burgeoned into the scene, and with it the need to structure the American university. This was a momentous decision! It would dictate who would attend, what they could achieve and the direction of societal progress. After much debate, the shortlist of its core focus was the liberal arts, practical training, and research—the latter two generated profits supported by the government, while the first gave students the foundational knowledge needed to make sense of the world. Instead of picking one, they decided to create a fourth option—all of the above.

The person who influenced this outcome the most was Charles Eliot. He believed that the old model of uncoordinated curricula would be worthless in daily life, and that the three ideas could exist in symbiosis. Harvard University, which had just happened to lose its third president in fifteen-years, was intrigued by Eliot's vision and hired him as president. Major structural change followed.

He began by making the bachelor's degree a requirement for admission into the graduate school. A side-effect of which was a large new market of undergraduate education, which they then promptly served. This was followed by making the PhD mandatory for teaching undergraduate liberal arts, and replacing the undergraduate mandatory curriculum with the elective system. He believed in *academic freedom*, i.e., instead of telling students what to learn, he let them choose. Consequently, this allowed the graduate and undergraduate schools to coexist. You see, the graduate school's primary goal is research. Professors have complete authority as to what they may pursue, so specialization is commonplace, and with that, the ability to teach only within those narrow boundaries.

Such niche professors would've been utterly useless in the old model. When the curriculum is standardized and only a couple pages long, little human capital is needed. But, with the electives model, everything flipped—the more professors a school has, the larger array of electives they could offer.

Naturally, other institutions saw the positives of this model and swiftly adopted it. And thus began the dynasty of the modern university. To give perspective on the speed of proliferation, the first American Ph.D. was awarded in 1861. Within three decades, it became the gold standard of credentialing in academia.[34]

This is how the university we are familiar with today came to be—an institution designed to facilitate three very discrete outcomes. In theory, it seemed like a wonderful solution. But that's the problem, it only worked in theory. The drawbacks of this strange hybrid have been facing criticism ever since its inception.

Let's begin with the PhD as a requirement to teach. Right from the get-go, philosopher William James, who taught at Harvard for a fantastic forty-four years, questioned this system. In his essay titled *The Ph.D. Octopus,* he wrote,

> Will anyone pretend for a moment that the doctor's degree is a guarantee that its possessor will be successful as a teacher? Notoriously, his moral, social, and personal characteristics may utterly disqualify him for success in the class-room; and of these characteristics his doctor's examination is unable to take any account whatever...The Ph.D. degree is in point of fact already looked upon as a mere advertising resource, a manner of throwing dust in the Public's eyes.[35]

He was ignored.

Fast forward forty years, and the same message was echoed by historian Jacques Barzun in his book, *Teacher in America.*

> The doctorate of course shows nothing about teaching ability.[36]

Once again, the same reaction—and nothing has changed since. These assertions remain as valid today as they were a century ago.

As an extension to this, we move on to the electives.

A PhD in what? Teaching?

For research, professors were state-of-the-art. For teaching, they were anything but. Still, under Eliot's staunch belief in academic freedom, professors were given complete autonomy in designing courses. The following is important to understand. The university has no particular rationale as to why it offers the courses it offers. It does so only because the professor has some background in that field. Happy to oblige, professors create and teach these courses with minimal oversight from superiors and no coordination amongst departments across institutions. This last point is borderline comical. In 2012, American higher education institutes granted 140,000 bachelor's degrees in business administration, 103,000 in general psychology, 50,000 in Accounting, 94,000 in nursing and 39,000 in political science.[37] For such universally popular fields, it's very hard to justify splendid isolation across institutions—unless, of course, it would expose the inabilities of the expert researcher-amateur teacher.

The credit-hour system, too, is deeply flawed. It is the embodiment of time-based methodology to measure learning (for which chapter 16 exposes all its weaknesses). For now, I will end by quoting Robert Hutchins, who served as president of the University of Chicago.

> The intellectual progress of the young is determined by the time they have been in attendance, the number of hours they have sat in classes, and the proportion of what they have been told that they can repeat on examinations given by the teachers who told it to them… [I]t is clear that these criteria are really measures of faithfulness, docility, and memory; we cannot suppose that they are regarded as true indications of intellectual power.[38]

Today, we finally see even the arbitrary adoption of the four-year course of study coming under fire. Sure, four years wasn't necessarily a bad system when it was conceived, but its weaknesses are now becoming increasingly visible with each passing day. Today, for most, it's far more effective to learn the fundamentals, and then absorb a nuanced understanding of the subject *on the job*. Things are simply moving way too fast in the world we live in for one to waste a year or two in the name of preparation. I'm not against preparation, I'm against lying to yourself.

This is critical: in an attempt to create a symbiotic system that facilitates three discrete outcomes, the inadvertent net winner was the research university. The institution's structure evolved to become one that turned a blind-eye to teaching and set all incentive structures based on quality of work done in the research laboratory—for example, quotas for research publications—not classrooms. These serve the researchers, while marginalizing learners. As the historian, Laurence Veysey wrote,

> The most pronounced effect of the increasing emphasis upon specialized research was a tendency among scientifically-minded professors to ignore the undergraduate college and to place a low value on their function as teachers.[39]

If it's not clear already, with the singular focus of producing more research, we have ourselves a conflict of interest. To bring down costs for the student, schools could easily adopt curriculum, lectures and supplemental material for popular majors, especially with the technology available today. But if they did, why would they need large departments full of professors? The same number of students could be catered to by fewer professors. But that would mean less potential for research output—unacceptable! Coupled with the professors' full authority of the classroom and their obvious willingness to keep themselves employed, we end in a situation where universities actively avoid being efficient. The incentives are structured to want more professors, not less. Suffice to say, they don't advertise this inconvenient truth.

More than anything, it's a design problem. One that is causing universities to fail at accomplishing its fundamental purpose—student learning. Yet, we see them everywhere! They follow the mentality of 'everyone's using it, so it must work,' and we're buying into it because of the same flawed rationale.

∽

The obvious next question becomes, how has this weird system survived for so long in spite of all its drawbacks?

For one, in the early days of the university, exclusive access only permitted well-off highly intelligent individuals. This insulated faculty, who neglected teaching, from exposure as the brightest of the bunch could find workarounds in the form of self-education. Also, for those aspiring to be scholars themselves, a professor's inability to teach could easily be compensated for by a thorough understanding of the subject. Not to mention, by giving full-classroom authority to professors, it obfuscated the measure of quality. As outcomes were determined by the professors themselves, they could eradicate evidence exposing their inadequacies by simply re-defining student-learning outcomes, year after year.

Next, emerging institutions needed to represent themselves as legitimate if they were to become established. What better way than to mimic existing ones? Additionally, this perpetuated the formation of two very influential classes: administrators and professors. With the goal of sustenance, each promoted the status quo. And considering that advancements in their careers often meant moving to a different institution, it was critical that they were structurally similar to make the move as frictionless as possible—for all parties involved. A perfect example of Parkinson's Law—bureaucracy creates more bureaucracy.

Over time, the system benefitted through habit—people just got used to doing things a certain way. Entire systems and processes were built around higher education being the way it is now—a path for high school graduates, employer expectations for freshers, HR practices built around them, etc. It's always more difficult to go against inertia. And if the Ph.D. shows nothing about teaching ability, then what?

Now, none of this guaranteed the hybrid model's existence at the scale it did. Isomorphism is often the reason behind the slow death of large successful companies. However, in the case of higher education, more than a century has passed, and it has failed to claim its victim. Why?

Well, in addition to what I just mentioned, there were larger forces at play—for various reasons, supply and demand just kept going up. This is what we will cover in the rest of this chapter.

Uncle Sam

The government played its part in two ways. First, through the distribution of massive research grants.

In July of 1945, President Truman received a report from the National Office of Scientific Research and Development, titled *Science: The Endless Frontier*. It read,

> In 1939 millions of people were employed in industries which did not even exist at the close of the last war—radio, air conditioning, rayon and other synthetic fibers, and plastics.... But these things do not mark the end of progress—they are but the beginning if we make full use of our scientific resources.
>
> The publicly and privately supported colleges, universities, and research institutes are the centers of basic research. They are the wellsprings of knowledge and understanding. As long as they are vigorous and healthy and their scientists are free to pursue the truth wherever it may lead, there will be a flow of new scientific knowledge to those who can apply it to practical problems in Government, in industry, or elsewhere.[40]

It called for massive federal investment in research. Considering the advantages of scientific progression were made explicit by the end of WWII, the money promptly found its way into the universities, effectively becoming a significant revenue stream.

The second role the government played was providing college subsidies.

In an effort to avoid a repeat of the Bonus Army march of 1932—in which WWI veterans protested for months after their return as employment was hard to come by—the G.I. Bill was passed. It gave soldiers returning from WWII financial aid to attend colleges.[41] Additionally, several legal initiatives, such as the 1954 Brown vs. Board of Education verdict, catalyzed the growth of minority groups aspiring for a college education, for whom the Higher Education Act of 1965 provided subsidized student loans (now known as Pell Grants). At first glance, both these instances seem to have done their job, but the second and third-order consequences proved to be devastating.

With respect to the research grants, the key factor is that the government didn't choose who to fund based on teaching ability—there was a global race of science and technology to be won at all costs. Universities saw this trend and began the necessary expansion to attract the billions being handed out. Again, students bore the brunt of this.

As for the loans, things get a bit muddy. They definitely solved the immediate issue at hand—veterans, people of colour, women and minority groups were given the opportunity to attend college. But over time, the emergent regulations and practices surrounding it have made it a nightmare for the millions who've taken out these loans.

The most important point to note is the non-existent consumer protection. When you can't pay back credit card debt, you can file for bankruptcy. When you can't pay back a mortgage, you can file for bankruptcy. When you can't pay back pretty much any loan, you can file for bankruptcy. But when it comes to college loans? NO, they're special. You can't file for bankruptcy. They stay with you for the rest of your life. This is quite literally the definition of indentured servitude! Lifelong at that. We thought slavery had been abolished long ago, but it turns out, there's a loophole.

Knowing this, it's crazy to see how easy it is to receive student loans. Lenders don't check credit-worthiness, the field of study being financed, earning potential, academic performance, nothing! The worse a candidate appears on paper for a traditional loan, the better they are for the student loan.

Why do lenders throw money at people who have no chance of paying it back? Well, it's all backed by the government. The agencies aren't fronting the bill! They're just facilitating the exchange. It is the government that is supplying the billions of dollars. The net effect of which is a system that has allowed people who shouldn't be going to college, to go to college, and simultaneously be set up to fail. The act of loaning isn't the problem, it is targeting those who can't pay it back—predatory lending at its best.[42]

Considering, not once in the education system—K-12 or higher—is financial literacy emphasized, the entire system looks a bit premeditated. Sure, one can learn this on their own or from friends and family, but no one in their right mind can deny that there's something incredibly fishy about this whole situation—the government not enforcing financial education, and then throwing money at financially ill-educated minds who lack understanding about the life-crippling effects of debt.

Of course, not all loans are the same, but most eighteen-year-olds won't do the due diligence necessary of parsing through the Costco receipts, that is the Loan Terms and Conditions, in spite of it being a monumental life decision. They are far too addicted to the idea of college; the portrayal of college beckons indulgences. The fundamental problem here is the teenager's inability to internalize the maxim, short-term sacrifices for long-term gains. And can you blame them? They've barely lived, and by definition, to experience the effects of long-term gains one needs to let time pass for a *long term*.

At the end of the day, federal aid is insulating colleges from having to take market-driven cost-cutting measures. They don't need to be efficient since the money keeps flowing, which further drives up costs. In a world without government interventions, raising prices above middle-class affordability would lead to the loss of millions of customers, but in our world, price hikes are being met with everybody just taking more loans.

Here, we transition to the next point—our culture.

Culture + Herd Parenting

The fact that college has been idealized by authority figures our entire lives is no secret. And their judgment deeply affects our decisions in inconceivable ways, especially when we go against conformity.

It starts in kindergarten. If a parent decides not to follow the traditional educational path for their child, they are the *others*. The same happens as we approach adulthood—those who don't go to college are considered inferior. All high schools have college resources of some sort, so *clearly*, college must be the correct route post-high school. Simultaneously, for some, parental pressure makes the whole ordeal more of an obligation rather than a decision. Yes, most parents mean well. When they nudge their child towards college, it is with the intention of protecting them from paths that often lead to limited opportunities. Not to mention that a college education worked out for their generation, so the idea that it works for all is deeply ingrained. However, there are some who only do so to fulfil their need to compete in social circles. To them, their kid's achievement is *their* achievement, and they end up sacrificing their child's future in the process.

Keep in mind, this is all during a time in a student's life when they have nothing figured out! So when people start asking, 'what are you going to do?' and we have no answer, insecurity creeps in. College, then, becomes an easy fix—it is literally advertised as direction for the directionless. This decision is further encouraged by prominent figures all over media, pushing a pro-college message. Former US President, Bill Clinton, is fond of pointing out that, 'More and more people with specialized skills are finding good jobs.'[43] Even Barack Obama said, 'Higher education is the single best investment you can make in your future.'[44] Clearly, neither are explicitly advocating for the traditional four-year college, they're just stating the need for more education. But the majority always generalizes and misinterprets these sentiments into prioritizing college. With that, the decision of student loans becomes a no-brainer. And of course, when we see all our friends doing the same, we end up being bombarded with a narrative that normalizes the whole ordeal—look around, everyone else is doing it! We try to make it seem as if it was our decision, but it never really was. We were primed for it.

∽

- In 2012, 41 per cent of all Americans 18 to 24-years-old were in some form of degree-granting program.[45]
- In 2009, 70 per cent of all American high school graduates were in college. The highest amount in U.S. history.[46]

∽

Further, those who've already got their degrees, in their effort to rationalize the great opportunities lost by going to college, often put it on a pedestal—not everyone, obviously, but a significant number. This is clearly seen when they use their degree as validation for them being educated. To state the obvious, claiming to be educated only because you went to college is like saying that you're in shape today because you worked out diligently from age eighteen to twenty-two. In reality, such claims are nothing more than a superficial bandage for the deep wound that is an inadequate understanding of the world. Because, for them, learning stopped the day they graduated.

On top of everything, we are repeatedly told that thinking about money when picking a career path is wrong. Which, in essence, I don't completely disagree with, but this mentality, in college, incorrectly gets extrapolated to, 'don't consider money when picking what to study.' We've made valuing money taboo! Dangerous. There's a certain degree of ignorance that young humans consistently display of the past and future. We give the present utmost value, ignoring the fact that the future will be our present someday. And so, students choose their field of study based on impermanent feelings, making much bigger bets than they can afford, at the expense of their future quality of life.

At the core is the false assumption that everyone should go to college, followed by the notion that an enjoyable college experience is worth *any* cost. For example, a family earning about $75,000 should not send their child to a college that charges half their annual income. But if they want to, the ever-present loans have allowed them to do so. And the reality of the situation is that many kids know that they have debt, but it hasn't registered. They don't associate themselves with it—it's free money for *'future me'* to worry about. They haven't revolved around the sun enough to understand debt's impact. Needless to say, these are the perfect conditions for the emergence of the debt trap.

Learning art history, for example, is great, but I don't understand why people wrack up debt for it. No doubt, it's a great goal to work towards, but not as the answer to a decision that will influence the rest of your life. And it's just not art history. We see so many people earning their degrees in fields which have incredibly low employment potential—and even less chance of repaying their student loans. I'm not saying go into any field just because it's hot right now. I'm saying, if a loan must be taken, be aware that it creates a big ditch to get out of, and the materials learned will heavily influence your ability to escape from that ditch. Never forget Bryan Caplan's words.

> You're more likely to find a major you love than a job that uses the major you love.[47]

Post graduation, when the monthly payments start to outpace their earning's growth trajectory, graduates are forced to make decisions that aid in short-term relief at the expense of their long-term growth. This, naturally, further increases the gap between their earning's growth and monthly payments. Leading to a negative feedback loop that grows exponentially as interest compounds. This is the debt trap. There are some who take the debt, get a job, pay the debt, and have a great life. There are many more who don't.

∽

The world is getting ever so complicated day-by-day. I get it. There are so many things going on that it's not only mentally exhausting but also time-consuming to update our understanding of society so we may navigate our lives more effectively. But this is no excuse when it comes to education. Education is one of the few things that an individual can do to actively move towards accomplishing whatever goals they may have.

Now, in spite of the great number of resources available to those privileged enough to be alive today, I don't expect high school graduates—kids whose brains are not physiologically fully developed—to understand the implications of their decisions and rationally execute on the best course of action.

This is where I believe parents need to do a much better job. As I said, the world is complicated, but I don't think many parents put in the necessary work to aid in a productive discussion about their child's future.

'College worked for my generation, so it must be the right decision,' is the mentality most have; and it spreads like cancer.

Another group of parents make it a point to visit college counsellors, often before the question of, 'if college is the right option,' has even been considered. Now, not all counsellors are bad, but their job literally depends on college being the popular choice for further education.

So, of course, they are going to advocate for it! One point to note: if you come across one that makes you do a short personality test, and then attempts to plan your entire future within an hour's meeting, RUN! Do not be duped into paying huge amounts of money to get the superficial feeling of preparation. Nobody, *I repeat, nobody* can figure out your path in life in one-sitting—this is often a lifelong process.

In any situation, this parental herd mentality is dangerous and must be stopped. Parents, at a time when all the world's information is at your fingertips, you're obligated to learn about the reality that is in play *today*, and further impart this knowledge to your child. Nothing less is acceptable—especially if you're not fronting the bill.

I'm aware many might've felt attacked by this section, so I want to end by saying this: I know it's difficult when all the evidence points towards the fact that we've made a mistake—I've been there, especially when that one decision has had so much influence on the life we live today. Even more so when the topic at hand is education. Our education has shaped us. To question it is to question who we are. This is a Herculean line of inquiry for anybody. I don't have a sure-fire remedy to make it any easier, but the following has helped me.

Accept the truth while identifying and treasuring the positives. What we mustn't do is indulge our need to rationalize past mistakes by propagating our delusion onto the next generation.

College, the business

Just to be clear, there's nothing wrong with operating as a business. But if colleges are doing so, they should be treated like one as well.

Naturally, the first step is to prove that they do conduct operations like a for-profit organization. We've already covered their relentless pursuit of revenue generation to plow into expansion, so I won't talk about that. Instead, we'll start with a quote from Susan Fournier, the Dean of Questrom Business School at Boston University (a registered private *non-profit* institution).

> Interviewer: 'This [the school] is a business?'
> Dean: 'It is a business'[48]

But other than word-of-mouth evidence, it is also evident in their actions.

Advertising. *The advertising is absurd.* The incredible amount of money spent to sensationalize the college experience can, and very easily does, persuade naive children to envision college as an inevitable part of their lives. Granted that a lot of this is done by independent media, but that doesn't get colleges off the hook for the deceiving ads that end up targeting people who can't afford the large risks involved. For example, many advertising messages make it a point to drop in phrases like, '97% of our graduates are employed within a year of graduation.' But they will never reveal that *employed* could mean a part-time gig or a minimum wage job, something that doesn't need a degree.[49]

Textbooks. A scam inside a scam! Colleges are literally juicing students for every dollar of revenue! There's a term for this in business called reducing the customer acquisition cost. Case in point: a professor makes a textbook mandatory, the student buys it for $200 from the school, the school buys the book back (at the end of the semester) for pennies on the dollar, and then the school resells it to the next poor batch of sheep at full price. All along, the total cost per book for the university was around $5—that's a 40x markup on a *mandatory* book! I'll leave it up to you to decide if this sounds like a scam or not.[50] This isn't a one-off instance. According to data from the Bureau of Labor Statistics, from January 1977 to June 2015, textbook prices have increased a whopping 1,041%—three times over the rate of inflation.[51]

Guaranteed admission. Some schools offer guaranteed admission for students, solely based on high school academic credentials. At first glance, this seems to provide deserving students with the opportunity to receive a college education, but as soon as the ineffectiveness of grades and test-based scores are revealed (discussed in Chapter 16), it is easy to see how this is a hindrance to those who also deserve a college education but aren't stereotypically smart. Regardless of it being a net-positive or negative, it definitely helps the colleges. They are guaranteed a steady supply of students. In the business world, this is known as keeping your sales pipeline full.[52]

In tandem to guaranteed admissions, there is also the rise of merit-based aid. That is, financial aid based on factors other than a student's financial circumstance. Once again, at first glance, this seems to be a harmless incentive for students to work hard in high school. And, even though it does succeed in doing so, it creates a second-order consequence of less financial aid going to students who *actually* need the money. And the funny thing is that an increasing amount of these funds are coming out of the pockets of the colleges themselves, not the public sector. Why do colleges do this? It serves two purposes, (1) keeping the sales pipeline full, and (2) attracting students with higher test scores. These, in turn, boost the college's position in the aforementioned rankings. I am a perfect example of this. I, who neither applied for nor needed financial aid, was offered 50 per cent off my tuition bill from a school I had applied to. Being an international student, if I'd taken the offer, it would've been north of $100,000 that could've been used to help students who genuinely needed the same financial aid.

Legacy admission. Let's not forget about their customer loyalty program. I won't go into much detail about how this acts as a huge barrier for low-income students to access higher education. It's obvious. All in all, it is but one more instance that makes the current higher education system only an illusion of meritocracy.[53]

Funnily enough, this *commercialization* is manifest on both sides: schools are acting like businesses and students are responding as customers. In fact, many of the points discussed in the *Ideological*

Inbreeding section arguably stem from this. Why else would university presidents, without any resolve, accept ultimatums from misbehaving students? Why would leadership across the university system willingly turn a blind eye to the disruption of free speech and other behaviour that violates their own codes of conduct?[54] This seems more like customer service than anything else to me. As Eric Adler, professor at the University of Maryland, said in a 2018 article,

> Campus intolerance is a problem for the free exchange of ideas. But the fundamental cause isn't students' extreme leftism or any other political ideology. It is a market-driven decision by universities, made decades ago, to treat students as consumers— who pay up to $60,000 per year for courses, excellent cuisine, comfortable accommodations and a lively campus life.

He goes on …

> Even at public universities, 18-year-olds are purchasing what is essentially a luxury product. Is it any wonder they feel entitled to control the experience? … Students, accustomed to authoring every facet of their college experience, now want their institutions to mirror their views. If the customers can determine the curriculum and select all their desired amenities, it stands to reason that they should also determine which speakers ought to be invited to campus and what opinions can be articulated in their midst. For today's students, one might say, speakers are amenities.[55]

To rub salt into the wounds, the numbers corroborate a trend towards spending on lifestyle amenities in an effort to attract more revenue.

∽

- From 2003 to 2013, across all types of higher education institutes, the average spending for instruction rose 7.7 per cent, research declined by 4.3 per cent, while student spending

> spiked 20.6 per cent.[56]

- As case-in-point, take Louisiana State University's 536-foot-long lazy river in the shape of the school's letters. Paid for with $85 million in student fees. *Eighty. F*cking. Five. Million. Dollars.*[57] As many have aptly described, today, campuses look more like country clubs than places of study.[58]

Okay, now that we've established how colleges function like businesses, here's where things get messy.

As we saw earlier, there are two customer bases that universities cater to—researchers and students. Now, like I briefly mentioned, a point that they don't like talking about is that this inherently creates a conflict of interest. The better the researcher, the more federal money comes in. This results in professors being hired because of their ability to research rather than to teach. As you would assume, organizing a growing number of professors, each doing their own thing, is not a very efficient business model. With the elective system, however, each professor, regardless of how esoteric his field, could be brought into the school to research *and* teach. Allowing schools to bring in large numbers of professors without increasing net expense, as they can now market the large and diverse class offerings to justify further tuition hikes.

Additionally, tenure exacerbates this entire situation. See, institutions compete in the academic community to attract celebrity professors, which increases the college's worth in the academic community. To expedite this feedback loop, colleges offer lifelong job security. I'm not against paying professors what they deserve, but what tenure often does is make professors lazy with regards to teaching, as they were never interested in doing so in the first place. They came for research. They see teaching as a chore.

It's all incredibly ironic; there is no such thing as tenure in medicine, and that is for good reason. If a doctor starts slacking, we can't afford to send them into the field—someone's life is at risk. The same argument is true in education, but is conveniently overlooked. The fact of the matter is, education tends to have an equal effect on one's life; difference is that the repercussions aren't immediately or tangibly visible. See, learning is quite literally the physical alternation of neurons, making education the intentional manipulation of the brain—it is brain surgery, and we're letting lazy surgeons perform it on thousands.

Next, since the vast majority of colleges are registered as non-profits, they don't pay taxes! I have no problem with colleges getting tax breaks. Without schools, we arguably don't have society. But the following is critical to understand. There is the school—the entity that performs the educational activities—and the endowment—the entity, essentially an asset management firm, that financially supports the school. So, we have schools with hundreds of millions (if not billions), employing financial professionals to grow their endowment yearly, completely tax-free. To be clear, this is not the problem. The problem is that these same schools then choose to prioritize growing their investment account over using it to help run the school that enabled them to get the tax breaks in the first place. I'll provide an example. Open the Books, an organization on a mission to make public spending more transparent, found that from 2010 to 2015, $41.59 billion of the Ivy League's revenue originated from the taxpayer. In other words, over the same time period, the average annual sum received by the Ivies from the taxpayer—$4.31 billion—exceeded the sum received by a third of the states in the USA! These schools have goddamn billions of dollars in their endowment, but still seem to need more. Again, I have no qualms with the concept of giving non-profit institutes of education tax breaks, but to run their operations, if they blatantly rely on not only the student to amass burdensome debt, but also the taxpayer to fund it, then they should be expected to pay their taxes as well.[59]

Most importantly, like in any industry, when there is an emergence of monopolistic traits, it often ends with the customer worse off. Education is no different. And, as it stands today, institutions of higher education have a rather ridiculous monopoly on accreditation.

In the late 1800s early 1900s, established institutions decided it was important to define what it meant to be a university. So they created non-profit accreditation organizations to do so.[60] On their board of directors? You guessed it, the incumbents.[61]

These *independent* organizations dictate who is allowed to enroll students (bringing with them billions of dollars in federal loans), who is allowed to receive billions more by the government in the name of research, where a student can transfer (so that previous class credits count) and, of course, who gets the tax breaks. As a result, if new institutions have any hope to compete on a level financial playing field, they are forced to adopt the current standards regardless of their inefficiencies. Thereby restricting innovation and similar competitive forces from exposing the faulty model. It's insane how this fact gets almost no media coverage.

Now, this wouldn't be that big a problem if the diploma wasn't important. But as we all know, that isn't the case. There just isn't another filtration mechanism as convenient and cost-effective for the employer as the college degree. All companies know that there are exceptional workers who didn't go to college, but it simply isn't worth the resources to find them. Thus emerged the degree as a mandatory requirement for employment.

Now, what this means in economic terms is that it made the college degree price inelastic. Time for Economics 101. Price elasticity is a measure of how reactive the demand for a good or service is to a change in price. If a product's demand is price inelastic, the demand will change less than proportionally to the change in price. Since there was no alternative to the college degree, *and* employers made it mandatory, ~~the diploma mills~~ colleges knew that even if they increase prices, people will have no choice but to still attain a degree. In other words, a huge change in price would mean a very small decline in college applicants. And that is exactly what we see—less than 10 per cent of the US population had a degree in 1960, more than 20 per cent in the 1970s, 25 per cent in the 1990s and around 33 per cent today—in spite of prices skyrocketing past any sane limit.[62]

In such circumstances—a large concentration of money and a great lack of accountability—as one would expect, we have corruption. Admission scandals and other legal investigations are on the news every day, and they even take place in reputed universities, such as Yale and Harvard.[63] This is not to say that such institutions provide no value, but to expose yet another symptom of organizations prioritizing clout and becoming too bureaucratic for their own good. Unfortunately, all the factors discussed in this section made it so that the burden of this toxicity fell on the student and taxpayer, while higher education institutions have gotten away scot-free.

15

What has college become?

As Mr Thiel likes to ask, 'How exactly do you describe your higher education?'

Is it an investment product, consumption product or an insurance product? It's helpful to answer this question because it helps put expectations in order. There may be some that can narrow it down to only one but I suspect that for many, it's all of the above. It was for me.

So, let's break them down individually to give an idea of why college isn't worth it for the majority, regardless of the lens through which we look at it.

College, the investment

One of the most commonly referenced tools when measuring an investment is Return On Investment (ROI). We've all heard the argument that in the long run, the returns of college will be much greater than its costs, thereby giving it a positive ROI. But the ROI metric does not take into account a very crucial element—Time. An investment can be ROI negative for ten years before becoming positive, and as life shows us often, a lot can happen in ten years.

∽

- Goldman Sachs found that the time taken for the typical student to break-even on the college investment is on the rise.[1]

- 2010 graduates won't break even until age 30
- 2015 graduates won't break even until age 31
- 2030 graduates won't break even until age 33
- 2050 graduates won't break even until age 37

∽

Another commonly referenced factor is the stark earning premium of a college graduate over a high school graduate. But there's a lot missing from the picture painted by this point of view.

First, while measuring the returns of college, the average outcome is irrelevant without considering the spectrum of possible outcomes. There are simply too many variables for each student to blindly follow the average outcome. As Wharton Professor Peter Capelli puts it,

> It would be like using the average temperature of the earth—
> fifty-five degrees—to decide whether to wear a coat today. It
> is a school-by-school story, perhaps even a major-by-major one
> within each school.[2]

Moreover, the positive correlation between a higher income and education is based on relative levels of education, not absolute ones. Christopher Caldwell summed it up well in the *Claremont Review of Books.*

> Those (our president included) who believe that everyone can
> receive today's college-level salaries if everyone can be sent
> to college do not understand how specialization works. They
> might as well argue that, because kickers score more points than
> offensive linemen, the best NFL team would have 53 kickers
> on it.[3]

Second, the statistics favouring the generous college pay-off are heavily skewed. For starters, it's more of a historical representation of college outcomes than that of current times. For example, the high earning college graduates—those who skew the average result upwards—are based on data points from those who graduated, on average, a decade ago.[4] Furthermore, when we discount the numbers from high paying fields and reputed schools, the numbers significantly drop. Not to mention, as touched upon before, the earnings post graduation is irrelevant to the payoff if the money and time needed for college is ignored. A more accurate measure would be if earnings would offset all incurred costs. Through this lens, the financial returns from many institutes appear to be negative, and that too before we take debt into the equation.

Third, the accuracy of return estimates for a complex investment, such as college, is highly dependent on what the variables are considered to be. I could be wrong, but I believe it was Bernard Russel who said,

Given an irrational assumption, you can deduce anything.

This, my friend, is fact.

For example, The Brookings Institution's Hamilton Project calculated the degree to have a 15 per cent return per year—beating almost all standard financial investments![5] This return, however, assumes there is no difference in a student who stops her education after high school as opposed to one who attains a college degree, the student graduates in four years (which is far from the standard), and that today's college wage premium will remain the same for every age group over their lifetime. In other words, when today's graduates turn thirty, they will earn just as much as those who are thirty today. This last assumption amuses me—it is exactly like saying that an investment will guarantee a return solely based on current and historic performance. If someone makes such an offer as an investment opportunity, he might very well find himself in jail. That's why Rule 156 of the Securities & Exchange Commission, to combat misinformation, makes it mandatory for investment companies to tell their investors not to base their future expectations on past performance before they invest. However, in education, such promises are commonplace.

More sophisticated analyses produce sobering estimates. *Payscale*, a juggernaut in the salary data aggregation space, teamed up with *Businessweek* and, based on more realistic assumptions, reported that almost 25 per cent of colleges had a negative return on investment! At such schools, the best path for the student is to leave.[6]

All in all, this makes college a very risky investment (as opposed to the safe option portrayed by conventional wisdom). But as we all know, college provides us with more than just numbers. There is intangible value provided to students through their various offerings. Unfortunately, there's a lot that colleges don't tell us about the realities of the *college experience*. So, I shall now present my case for why the benefits sold to us aren't as, well, existent, as we're led to believe.

Let's begin with the Networking argument.

Yes, this is true. Meeting the right people *can* happen on the college campus. Through not only alumni, but also existing employer-university ties. However, this value proposition decreases *significantly* the further down the college is on the prestige ladder. The potential to meet someone who can make a career is nowhere near the same in any run-of-the-mill mid-tier school as opposed to the Ivies and equivalents.

Additionally, there are many cheaper alternatives to expand your network. From online solutions such as LinkedIn, to physical meetups such as conferences and seminars. These can cost a few hundred up to a thousand dollars, but they are much safer bets to achieve your objective.

It is also important to note that as much as college can connect students with the right people, it holds the potential to expose students to those who can drag them down. Peer pressure, or social conformity in general, are very real factors when we talk about the human being. Ironically, the chance of this negative effect significantly *increases* as we go down the college prestige ladder. This is less likely to happen at events specifically scheduled for the purposes of networking.

Second, the Self-Discovery argument.

I'll be the first to admit, one can definitely learn a lot about themselves on a college campus. The opportunity to dabble in an extraordinary variety of events, activities, subjects, etc. is hard to come by, especially when we consider the proximity of one facility to another. Alas, the extent to which this feature is marketed is absurd.

Let's start with clubs and activities. They cost money…not what you pay for as tuition, but additional fees such as registration, participation, membership, etc. There's nothing wrong here but why are we paying $20,000 a year (at the least) *for the option* to pay more for what was sold as a package deal? This is not a deal breaker or anything of the sort, but I find it a bit deceptive; even though some charges are as low as $20-$30, like those for intramural sports, some can cost up to a few hundred dollars *per semester,* like those to join clubs of any kind.

Next, electives—the opportunity to try out a diverse array of classes. We've already gone over all that is wrong with the upper-division electives, but there's also an element of misconception regarding electives as a whole. In a nutshell, the immense variety of classes offered creates an illusion of opportunity as we make the superficial connection between the great number of classes available to the great potential for students to try different things. Here, we miss out on two very important elements—quality and accessibility.

Let me break it down further.

The insane variety of classes available makes it incredibly difficult for students to successfully pick those that actually have the impact we all wish for them to have. Think about it like a menu at a restaurant. Would you rather have one with extensive options of questionable quality, or choose from a limited variety of tried-and-tested dishes? The inconvenient truth is that the large class offerings make the maintenance of a quality standard in the classroom almost impossible. While one professor in the Philosophy department may truly be conveying the merits and utility of philosophy, the act of trying to add classes to incorporate every student inevitably leads to degradation of learning outcomes as subpar teachers are hired. It's naive to think all teachers are made equal.

The large number of students competing for a limited amount of seats in the better professor's class exacerbates the situation. Especially now, as colleges can't wait to accept more students than in the previous year. This problem is so evident that we have websites such as *RateMyProfessor.com*, that allow students to review and rate their experience with a professor like a product on Amazon. It is now commonplace for students to look up these ratings before registering for any class. And when students encounter professors who haven't been rated, registration turns into a high-stakes gamble with their time and tuition money. For many, the odds of a positive outcome are so low that most would settle for a class that they can just pass.

This, coupled with the system of registration, truly makes it a disaster. In college, the time when a student can register for classes is dependent on how many credit hours he has completed. In other words, the more classes passed, the earlier a student can register. Consequently, it is the younger students who pay the price of this system. We are told we are free to try anything we want for the first two-years, without committing to a path until the tail-end of the second year. But what good does trying different topics do if they are taught by professors who don't convey the true essence of those subjects? You see, the growing number of accepted applications, plus older students being able to register first, inadvertently fills up all the good classes before the younger students can get a chance to register. When they do eventually rack up enough credits to get into the class they wanted, and do end up enjoying what they learned, it is often already year-three, where the option to switch their course of study is not without additional resource costs.

Surprisingly, and most comically, the many options advertised

A wide variety of topics available (?)

aren't always available. Since each class is designed by the professor in isolation, he has no authority over the prerequisites required to get into his class. In other words, if, for whatever reason, a prerequisite is unavailable to a student, then by default, all classes that require it become unavailable as well. If we discount for such situations, the range of classes one may freely register for is far smaller than what is actually advertised.

To be fair, in the pre-internet days, the argument for electives as they exist today still held up. But now, if the goal is only to figure out if the subject material is of any interest, students can just dabble. The material is available online!

What about learning to live independently and meeting people from diverse backgrounds? You know, dorm life and whatnot.

Well, again, this is true. But, the people who use this rationale to justify the cost are a perfect example of naive rationalization. Personally, I found the infamous *dorm experience* to be nothing more than a fad. Neither does one need to live in a dorm to grow up, nor do they need it to meet interesting people. In reality, dorm life is the highlight of very few people's college journey and even fewer would volunteer to go back there again. And the cost element makes the whole deal such a rip-off. Why would anyone pay upwards of $10,000 a year,[7] when with the same amount of money, one can live in several countries all over the world for many months? This would teach a student more about independence and also introduce them to people with more experience than what their wildest imagination could conceive of. When people truly learn and understand how far the same amount of money can take them, only then will they wake up to the opportunity cost they are incurring every single year. Sure, it won't be the most comfortable experience in the stereotypical sense, but that's part of the experience! That is, if growing up is the primary objective. (I recommend reading *Vagabonding* by Rolf Potts, as a starting point, if this is of interest.)

Next, the Liberal Arts argument.

What I refer to as the Liberal Arts is not a complete course of study classified under the Liberal Arts umbrella, but the general education/core curriculum that is mandatory for all. That said, nobody in their right mind would argue against the value of the liberal arts. Critical Thought, Articulate Communication, Questioning Timeless Truths, and other such abstract but essential skills are introduced and developed here. These are skills employers find most useful in high-level decision-making, but the hardest to inculcate into employees, especially those further along in their careers.

In theory, this should be one of college's strongest selling points. Even more so moving into the future, as this will be what determines one's ability *to learn how to learn*. Unfortunately, the institution of Liberal Arts faces two main issues. First, the same problem that plagues the electives—the decrease in quality of learning outcomes as quantity of class offerings increase. I'm not going to go any further with this as I have already made my point. Second, the method through which this material is taught.

Most classes look indistinguishable from any other. A professor lectures, students passively listen, take notes, the teacher says, 'feel free to ask any questions,' nobody asks any questions (except, of course, what and when the exam is), students take the exam, and receive a grade to determine how much they have learned. The issue is, when it comes to subjects like Philosophy, History or the Theory of Knowledge, the only way for students to truly reap the benefits is if they are curious to learn about it *themselves*. This is because the value of these subjects is not as evident as those that qualify a student for a job. It becomes clear only with time, as life goes on. So, when students can't see the purpose of what is being taught, they default to the mindset: 'the only thing that matters is that I pass the class'. This is why nobody asks questions! In essence, such subjects must be first *sold* to students.

The drawbacks of one's inability to teach cannot be more evident than in the Liberal Arts subjects. And considering the glut of professors who can't teach, it's no surprise that studies are producing results that show students are learning less and less.[8]

∽

- The Department of Education study tested for adult literacy by asking college-goers to perform tasks such as to draw inferences from different pieces of text, compare and contrast them, etc.[9]
    - In 1992, 40 per cent were considered proficient.
    - In 2003, 31 per cent were proficient, and only 14 per cent achieved basic literacy.
- In a 4-year study of a diverse variety of American colleges, 45 per cent of students made no gains in widely used tests of critical thinking, analytical reasoning and communication skills during the first two-years. And more than 33 per cent made no significant gains over the entire four years. The researchers wrote, 'American higher education…is characterized by limited-to-no learning for a large proportion of students'.[10]
- The non-profit, Organization for Economic Co-operation and Development, published a study which compared literacy, numeracy, and problem-solving of adults in different countries. 38 per cent of US college grads scored 2 or below on a 5 level assessment of numeracy involving problems with basic analysis of data and statistics.[11]
- In a study, researchers tested the effect of education on thinking skills by asking participants open-ended questions with no objectively correct answer. For example, 'Does violence in media cause violence in real life? What would the effects of a proposed law be?' The point was to observe the number of arguments used, the number of objections considered, the relevance of the answer and other such key

indicators. The findings: on a scale of 1 to 5, first and fourth-year college students both scored 2.8. In other words, four years of higher education had no effect on students' ability to reason.[12]

- Another study tested the ability of several hundred university students to apply methodological concepts to reasoning about everyday-life events. The author had this to say:

The results were shocking: Of the several hundred students tested, many of whom had taken more than six years of laboratory science in high school and college and advanced mathematics through calculus, almost none demonstrated even a semblance of acceptable methodological reasoning about everyday-life events described in ordinary newspaper and magazine articles. The overwhelming majority of responses received a score of 0. Fewer than 1% obtained the score of 2 that corresponded to a 'good scientific response.' Totally ignoring the need for comparison groups and control of third variables, subjects responded to the 'diet' example with statements such as 'It can't hurt to eat well'.[13]

- For what it's worth, my experience corroborates these findings.

చ

Lastly, the Job-skills argument.

Every time I think about this, I can't help but laugh. The first obvious drawback is the same that exists in the field of electives and Liberal Arts—a decline in the quality of learning as quantity of class offerings increase. More interestingly, for many professions, colleges are literally unable to teach relevant skills. Some classes may definitely be relevant, but describing the overarching curriculum as outdated is no stretch.

Primarily caused by the rapidly evolving landscape of technology and its ubiquity across every industry, the working world today is in a constant state of flux. Making the skills needed today look radically different from those that are needed tomorrow. The issue arises when the bureaucratic structure of college makes it near impossible for a syllabus change to be implemented within a relevant time-frame. More often than not, by the time the change is in effect, the working world has already transformed several times. And, *by chance,* if they do manage to teach skills that mirror what is being used in the workplace, the probability of them becoming obsolete by the time the student graduates is incredibly high. Time is the enemy of today's system of higher education. It is ridiculous that the stuff we learn as job skills in college can have little to no value by the time we graduate. There should be an explicit notice on every college application: 'WHAT YOU LEARN MIGHT BE OBSOLETE BY THE TIME YOU GRADUATE.'

This creates a very visible disconnect between employers and universities. Consequently, not only are many companies recognizing this and heavily investing in their own paths of higher education,[14] but also we see specialized courses and boot camps appear with resource costs much lower and teaching methods more efficient (relative to traditional higher education). Some even offer income-based tuition payments. In other words, 'You pay only if you get a job,' thereby eradicating the financial barrier altogether.

Skin in the game—this is another element about the college deal that should not be taken lightly. If your investment in a company tanks, it's also the company that suffers. However, if your investment in college doesn't result in the advertised benefits, it makes absolutely no difference to the college. Their cash flow is already secured. It's funny, in 2008 everybody lost their minds when the banks got hundred per cent of the profit while the individual took on hundred per cent of the risk. But now, nobody says a word when the colleges are receiving the same deal.

To conclude, the numbers are clear—on average, those with a college degree earn more than those without one. But the average doesn't account for a lot of important factors, which ends up giving us a very faulty perception of college outcomes.

Like professor Capelli puts it,

> The answer is that one size does not fit all... Think about the analogy with medicine. For every prescription drug, there is clear evidence that it has the desired effects on average, but we still require that every dose be administered by a licensed expert—your doctor—who has to decide whether the benefits of it in your situation are worth the potential side effects and increasingly whether those benefits are worth the financial costs of the treatment. When it comes to college, though, we have none of that expert guidance. We are asked to go with average results for the population as a whole.[15]

Like with any investment, it's all about probability, and a college graduate today is more likely to graduate with debt, than a job. Considering most people just want stability in their lives, college has become one of the last things one should pursue. As a result, unfortunately, those that need college to work the most are increasingly likely to end up in a worse situation—namely, deep in debt with no degree—than when they began. Education was meant to bridge the gap of unequal opportunity. Today, the bridge exists, but it's ridden with holes.

I hope it's clear by now that the college investment isn't really as good as we're led to believe, even more so when financed with debt. For every value proposition college offers, there are cheaper, more time-efficient and more effective alternatives in the market today. Use them, don't blindly follow what everyone else is doing.

Now, let's move on to insurance.

College, the insurance policy.

This is straightforward. It is the degree. To state the obvious: one needs to actually graduate to reap the benefits of this insurance policy. Unfortunately, some numbers don't lie.

႙

- About 60 per cent of students enrolled full-time in four-year programs will fail to finish in four years. The six-year graduation rate at public institutions is 60 per cent, 66 per cent at private non-profit institutions and only 21 per cent at private for-profit institutions! In other words, around 1 out of 3 college students won't graduate at all.[16] These numbers include top-tier colleges where graduation rates are significantly higher. If we discount them, the situation is worse.[17]
- Almost half of Americans begin higher-education at a two-year community college. Here, only 34 per cent either graduate or transfer to another school within three-years of enrolment.[18]
- Many enter community college with aspirations to earn a bachelor's degree. Only 11.6 per cent succeed within six-years.[19]
- About 1 in every 2 students pursuing an advanced degree won't finish it![20]

႙

The problems of the insurance policy don't end here! In fact, we're nowhere close. One of the main reasons that made the degree valuable—the lack of information—has pretty much done a complete 180. Today, information is everywhere.

As covered before, the degree signaled to the employer that the candidate has had exposure to information that was simply unavailable elsewhere. Now, however, all the world's information is accessible with an internet connection. This is a deceivingly new phenomenon. If we take the *dot-com* bubble as the inception of the internet as we know it today, it is quite literally just coming of age. Us kids feel like it's always been there, but that's only because we don't know what life feels like without it. Surprisingly, regardless of age, many can't seem to internalize its immense value. They see it as a gimmick, or at least a non-significant factor in the evolution of education. They don't understand what the internet is and/or choose to live in denial.

The internet is a medium through which one human shares information with another. At scale, when billions are connected, it democratizes information to a degree several orders of magnitude greater than anything else before it. This makes the internet a super-mind of sorts; a portal into the sum total of information accrued by billions.

Put another way—today, the same quantity of information an individual can be exposed to in one year, could easily have taken a decade to amass in the last century. (Read the sentence again, let it sink in, and ponder the implications of this degree of time savings.)

Its influence is comparable to the wheel, the spoken word, the printed word, the steam engine, electricity and all the great inventions that have made society what it is today.

Do you know the implications of this?

Well, there are many, but one is that no longer does knowledge have to be concentrated in physical locations, such as educational institutes or traditional libraries. Essentially, with access to the internet, anyone can learn almost anything, anywhere—an autodidact's dream come true.

No longer do colleges have a monopoly on the sophisticated forms of knowledge required for well-paying employment, and thus, for social mobility. Of course, we are still in early days, so it's still incredibly difficult to distinguish between fact and fiction, but within it lies the same information conveyed by teachers of all levels. With a stubborn will to filter through the clutter, it is not unheard of for the internet to be the primary source of one's education. It was for me. The answer to any possible question already exists online, the problem is finding it, and that's a problem we can solve. Only time stands in the way for internet self-learning to be as effective as physical colleges at price points much cheaper.

Technically, the information problem was solved a long time ago by Gutenberg. The only issue was that, relative to today's standards, it came with caveats. Books had to be physically stored, literacy was necessary and replication costs were high. The internet solved it all. Near infinite e-books can be stored on the cloud, the cost to replicate them is pretty much nil, and the rise of audiobooks and other long-form audio allows access to those who cannot read. Today, all information, past and present, can be stored, found and revisited forever.

The value of the diploma is falling.

There is no debate here. Of course, the degree to which an individual is affected depends on a lot of factors, such as the school's brand, course of study, etc. Nonetheless, we can make the following generalization: the millions—with blinders on, unintentionally or otherwise—who have trod along through moderately selective colleges, attaining generic degrees, *and are planning to rely on them,* are at risk. Historically, these degrees facilitated entrance into a category of the labour market highly in demand, not because of anything special about the piece of paper, but due to the absence of alternatives that conveyed the same information. Now, alternatives are presenting themselves, soon they will become mainstream and this will expose lack of learning. Nobody is going to care if you're the victim of an outdated societal belief. The floodgates of human potential are soon going to open and competition is going to be truly global. For perspective, as of 2020, less than half the world is connected to the internet, even fewer with a reliable connection.[21] This is going to change within our lifetime. Interestingly, this monumental shift is not lost on the colleges. They've recognized this and taken evasive action to ensure top-line growth.

I sometimes sympathize with higher educational institutes. On one hand, employers are quick to claim that new graduates are unfit to be hired, even though neither are they promising to hire anyone nor does their definition of fit remain constant for more than a couple years. And on the other hand, parents demand a guarantee that the many dollars and years spent in college will secure their child a good job—they seem to forget the wise words of one of the most influential college dropouts of our time.

'Nothing's ever promised tomorrow, today.'[22]

All along, the eighteen-year-old has not a clue in the world—to us, due diligence involves college rankings, the allure of the campus and maybe how the college tour guide treated us—that is, if we do visit. The best decision is *our* decision. The government is giving us free money for whatever we decide, so it must be that it will work out—*it has to*. Not to mention the four amazing years waiting for us as portrayed by the media, further clouding our already heavily misinformed decision.

To combat this, higher education's strategy of choice is abundantly evident—enrollment must stay up, so promises for employment continue to be dished out liberally. Resulting in a massive uptick of niche courses of study—named after job titles based on their best guess as to what employers might want. For example, Turf and Turfgrass Management programs at Ohio State and Purdue University, Golf Management at Florida Gulf Coast University, Adventure Education at Plymouth State University, Auctioneering at Harrisburg Area Community College, Bowling Industry Management and Technology at Vincennes University—the list goes on. They may sound like perfect opportunities to enter a new career path, but the outcomes have *not* been so perfect. None explicitly claim to guarantee a job, but their advertising doesn't leave much room for interpretation. For example, DeVry University frames it like this:

'Each year, thousands of our grads find themselves right where they want to be.'[23]

DeVry further reports that 100 per cent of their communications graduates secure a job within their field, six months post graduation. But they don't make it clear that what defines *in their field* includes those who had jobs before the program, and that they're only based on voluntary reports from around 80 out of 8000 total undergraduates.[24]

To be a responsible consumer, especially for products that demand large investment, the bare minimum is to look past marketing material and see if the numbers presented hold any water. When it comes to education, for some reason, we love gambling.

When we couple ignorant consumers with policy specifically aimed at boosting college attendance, it not only negatively affects the college graduate but also the non-degree holder—both, due to simple supply and demand.

First, let me explain why this is the case for the former. Like with money, when there is a sudden artificially created influx in supply, we have inflation. Similarly, as more people are getting a college degree and the employment opportunities that truly require it aren't proportionally increasing, the value of each individual degree is plummeting.[25]

Just to make it crystal clear, let me explain this phenomenon using an example. Imagine a full theatre. Now, the first row decides they want a better view, so they stand up. Which naturally prompts every row behind them to do the same, and we end up with no better visibility than when everyone was sitting down.

There are so many candidates with college degrees that betting on them just isn't as good a bet as it once was. When everybody is qualified, nobody is qualified. Yes, there are exceptions to this because not all degrees convey the same information. For example, a degree from an Ivy League school conveys that the candidate not only finished

"100% of our students get employed within a month of leaving college"

a rigorous course of study but also got through the admissions process in the first place. Sure, taking a chance on the Harvard grad is still worth it, but what about the candidate from a school you've never heard of before?

The fallacy of composition—the error of assuming that what is true for a member of a group is true for the group as a whole—is why degree inflation exists. People think just because the degree helped one person, it will help everyone equally. This is simply not true. Since the majority of the degree's value lies in what it signals to the employer, everybody earning one doesn't result in the same information being signaled, it changes what the signal means altogether.

Now, to answer why the oversupply of degree holders negatively affects the non-degree holders, we need to understand how the relationship between the diploma and the labour market has transformed.

The *college-to-lifetime career* at one company model began to erode in the early 1980s as large companies began to downsize and restructure, causing a surplus of degree holders into the labour market. Considering the explosion of experienced white-collar labourers, the maintenance of costly development programs became an unnecessary expense for many. As one CEO put it, 'Why should I train my employees when my competitors are willing to do it for me?'[26] Not surprisingly, in 2011, an Accenture survey of U.S. employees found that nearly 80 per cent received no employer-provided formal training in the previous five-years. The primary reason for which, of course, was that employers looked for precisely those employees that didn't require training.[27]

Moreover, to filter from the increased talent pool, hiring managers naturally start to increase job requirements. It is commonplace to see entry-level positions now requiring years of experience. So, the college grad gets a job—not the one they wanted, but a job nonetheless—and the high school grad gets stuck with a lower-level job, or in slow periods, no job. This is also why the *evidence* that the unemployment rate among college grads is significantly lower than that for high school grads is extremely misleading when judging the value of college. It isn't that there are many more jobs available for those with a college education, they just end up taking the jobs that would usually go to the high school grad.

Interesting, right?

(1) The price of the degree is going up while the value of what you get is falling, and (2) the amount of time spent in school needed *to get a job* has surpassed the amount of education needed *to do a job*. Both these reasons make the non-degree holders—especially those from lower socio-economic backgrounds—bear most of the brunt. In 1965, Lyndon Johnson said this,

> In a very few moments, I will put my signature on the Higher Education Act of 1965. ...It means that a high school senior anywhere in this great land of ours can apply to any college or any university in any of the 50 States and not be turned away because his family is poor.[28]

Unfortunately, the long-term effects of this policy has been the exact opposite of what was intended. Those educated in the field commented on this phenomenon.

> Relative to the 1990s, it is a future where even the demand for skilled workers is reduced. In this maturity stage, having a BA is less about obtaining access to high paying managerial and technology jobs and more about beating out less educated workers for the Barista or clerical job.[29]

The key takeaway here is, to earn a high-value insurance policy, one mustn't pursue degrees that are in demand *now*; they must be early in a field that is *going to be* in demand. This is infinitely more difficult. Students often pick a degree based on what's currently hot—the supply that entered the market while they're in school meets the surplus demand—and by the time they graduate, the degree has lost value—and that's best-case scenario. In today's world, skills don't become less valuable, they become obsolete.[30]

Education today, at least in the stereotypical sense, is a relatively small part of any job requirement, let alone of an individual's character—there are simply too many variables involved. Making college not as clear a stepping stone to a good job as it previously was. Hiring for experience over potential is the fundamental shift that is changing the relationship between traditional higher education and the labour market. Employers don't want to hire someone who needs to be trained, only those who can contribute immediately. And we see the impact of this ideological shift in college through the vast offerings in esoteric courses focused on practical training.

The unfortunate part is that colleges aren't being able to inculcate the practical skills employers want. The creators of curricula seem to ignore the few inputs employers give that remain constant. Considering the majority of students have gone to college to get a job, the answers of employers, when asked, were pretty, let's say, against the grain.

A survey of employers conducted by the National Association of Colleges and Employers, found *technical knowledge related to the job* was ranked 6 out of 9.[31] A similar survey conducted by the Chronicle of Education in 2013 showed that *work experience* was the key factor when employers were looking for an employee. So, for students who haven't had any kind of employment—internships or otherwise—their major was of little importance. In fact, the same survey showed that for employment that requires a degree, 70 per cent of employers would happily ignore the requirement if the candidate explicitly demonstrated the qualities they wanted.[32]

The disconnect is clear.

While colleges are advertising extremely narrow vocational courses as a path to good careers—and students blindly following this ideology—employer expectations are quite the antithesis.

Some schools have recognized this and have restructured curriculum to one that heavily focuses on internships and co-op programs. Considering the majority have gone to college primarily to get a job, this is good. However, it is important to note that, here, it is our tuition that's paying for the work experience—a hefty sum for many. Even though this is a step in the right direction, the existence of a growing number of cheaper alternatives—internships, income-based tuition boot camps, etc.—provides us with a dilemma, especially for those relying on a paying job post-graduation. Why go to college if the same outcome can be achieved elsewhere, without having to incur such a huge financial burden? This would also allow colleges to focus on what they do best—providing foundational knowledge that will be useful, potentially lifelong, as opposed to just for the first job. This is no trivial point. A career is a marathon, not a sprint. If college only helps obtain the first job, it's a pretty bad insurance policy.

∽

- Half of all college grads in 2010 and 2011 were unemployed or underemployed.[33]
- More recently, almost 66 per cent of graduates reported that they don't have a job that is closely related to their major.[34]
- More than 20 per cent reported that they received no information about the job market in college.[35]
- Almost 25 per cent already believe that their education was not worth the financial costs.[36]
- Among college graduates under 25:
    - 22.4 per cent are unemployed
    - 22 per cent are employed in fields that don't require a college degree.[37]
    - In 2010, 5700 janitors in the US had PhDs.[38]

∽

This *degree inflation*—the objective decrease in learning outcomes, and the instantaneous access to all information via the internet— has resulted in accreditation that once assured employment, to now become nothing more than a step through the door. The common belief that for a job—any job—college is a must, is simply not true anymore. What is needed is skill, and there are ever-increasing alternatives to acquire those. Small to mid-size companies, who happen to be the vast majority, don't care about the piece of paper because savvy employers know that no longer are the best employees, predominantly, products of the higher educational system. The largest companies in the world have begun to realize this and no longer make it necessary to hold a college degree to apply for a job. Bank of America, Google, Apple and IBM, to name a few.[39]

This is only the start. Similar to how a toy slinky falls[40] to the ground, this change will start at the top, and, over time, proceed to move downward. Despite it not seeming like it is at the bottom right now, it will be there soon enough.

College, the consumer good.

Looking back at myself four years ago, I must confess, this value proposition attracted me to college far more than I'd like to admit. I couldn't wait for the parties, the freedom and the whole shebang. And, I'm not surprised (see Chapter 14, section 'Culture').

Maybe it was my personality, or maybe something else, but the thought that, 'this is going to be the best time of my life' quickly (two years to be specific) disintegrated into disillusionment. I got bored; bored of doing the same thing every week, bored of drinking at every opportunity I got, bored of going to classes that I didn't care about, and under everything, a sense of inadequacy for not having anything to show for after two years. Especially during a time in human civilization where it has never been easier to create.

I noticed I was a minority in this realization and I was curious to know why. Unsurprisingly, the origins of this mentality can be traced back to K-12 education. An ideology has been drilled in so deep that many cannot distinguish it from reality. I don't think everyone has been brainwashed, but I can confidently say that a significant number have by a beautiful narrative that is, in essence, the following: the system says, attend twelve years of school, followed by four years of higher education, all to get a job—a safe job—a job wherein, if you put in the work and save the money, you can retire soon and enjoy the rest of your life with the people you love. In this beautiful narrative, they've constructed a place where you may be free, a place where you may have limitless fun, a place called college. They say, here, you're *allowed* to enjoy life to its fullest without a care in the world. *But,* only as long as you're in college. Binge-watch TV all day every day? Video games for hours at a stretch? Pushing the boundaries of your blood alcohol concentration? Don't worry about it, you're in college! There's an entire category now known as *party schools*—they know what they are and don't need to hide it. And you believe it, *I believed it,* because in this narrative they've given us a rationalization mechanism, which is, 'For the rest of your life, *you* are going to be working hard. *You* are going to give up fun for responsibility.'

To those that know what I'm talking about, let me offer a reality check.

The time period where a person should be having the most fun *is* in their twenties. It is this time period when a person can do whatever they want—fail, try again, fail *again* and so on. There is no other time in life where the potential for thrill is higher than it is now. *And in just two years,* colleges have the gall to allow just enough of that feeling so that a person succumbs to the mind-numbing predictability and monotony of the rat race.

I acknowledge that life is tough and some simply don't have the same opportunities, but for those attending college in the first world, they already have had more opportunities than literally 99 per cent of the world. This is no exaggeration. That number represents the truth. If we take the USA as an example, the largest first world country by population, there were around twenty million college-goers in 2019.[41] In the same year, the global population was around 7.7 billion.[42] If we simply divide the two, we get a mere 0.26 per cent. Isn't this privilege?

So, if we cut the amount of time we spend on recreational purposes in half, how much additional time would we have over the course of four years? Considering time spent on academics has fallen off a cliff, it most definitely is no small number.

∽

- A study published by the National Bureau of Economic Research found: in 1961, full-time college students spent 40 hours a week on college work. By 2003, this fell to 27 hours a week. More interestingly, 20 per cent of students themselves admitted to studying less than 5 hrs/week outside class (in the same period, 'A's given out increased from 15 to 43 per cent—a symptom of the falling standards. We will discuss this *grade inflation* in the next chapter).[43]
- The reason I bring this up is by no means to say that we need more school work—far from it. The fact that we are getting an increasing amount of time to ourselves is a blessing in disguise. That is, if we choose to utilize it correctly.

∽

So, let's reserve this time for doing something that will last. By which, I mean anything that survives past the physical occurrence of the act. Make music, create art, direct videos, do photography, research an industry, write a book, read a book, learn a skill, *learn anything you want!* All of which can be done with a smartphone or a computer and an internet connection. In the existence of all life *ever*, this is a very new opportunity that a great number of people undervalue.

Sure, you might not know what you really like or are good at, but only by forcing yourself *to do* will you gain the opportunity to figure it out, without which all you're left with is hypotheticals and theories. Our addiction to instant gratification has greatly blurred our vision as to what is possible in a single year. And, don't forget, we still have the other half to enjoy the freedom of not having burdensome responsibilities.

To conclude, I don't know how to meticulously deconstruct the stupidity of this reason for college because it isn't one that is explicitly used to justify the costs. But it bloody well is a reason why kids are addicted to the proposition of higher education. By no means am I saying college shouldn't be fun, but each person must decide if college as a consumer good is really worth the price. And please keep in mind, because we forget all too easily, parties, alcohol, drugs and everything else, are *not exclusive* to college!

16

All Our Years

Now, let's begin with a systematic dismantling of the major weaknesses that plague the education system in its entirety.

Too many well-intentioned, bad teachers

I must admit, this is a point I seriously contemplated leaving out. But whatever rationale I thought would justify doing so, none would change one thing—the fact that it's true.

On a quality-quantity x-y graph, the teaching profession is normally distributed. With terrible teachers on the left tail end—those who neither care nor possess the ability to teach—and great ones on the right—those who not only care deeply but also possess an intuitive ability to teach. But the vast majority are bang in the center. They represent the category I am talking about—those who care but are unable to guide students to the defined learning outcomes.

We must realize that teaching is an incredibly difficult task. Just as going to med school doesn't guarantee that one will be a good doctor, going to school to be a teacher definitely doesn't translate into becoming an effective catalyst for student learning. The teaching profession is an extremely nuanced and intricate dance of art and science; a good teacher possesses a sophisticated understanding of the material taught, an ability to think in a potentially infinite array of perspectives (often across cultures and several generations), articulate communication, and extraordinary patience. The affliction most teachers suffer from is their skillset stops at the first requirement. Unfortunately, that's the easy part. Anyone can learn the material. The issues start bubbling up when it comes time to impart said knowledge.

Why is it so?

To begin with, some simply have the wrong personality. For the same reason that everyone can't become a talk show host, not everybody is made to be a teacher. Considering that the education system is filled with many students who have no intention to learn, the first task a teacher must accomplish is getting the students enthused about the material. Learning is time and energy-intensive, and nobody wants to put work into something that doesn't reciprocate with value. Let me go further on this point.

The most common complaint heard amongst students of all ages is that there is no point in learning what is being taught, since it serves no purpose in the real world. I did this too. For many more cases than it should, this is true. However, over the years, I've realized that the content alone is not at fault. There are a whole host of topics that humans with the crutch of inexperience are simply unable to see value in. These include subjects like Philosophy, Psychology, Logic and so forth.

I want to make it abundantly clear: there is no fault in judging a class by its utility. The argument that learning is beautiful for its own sake is not one I wholeheartedly disagree with, but that point of view serves only a very niche population. The vast majority just want to attain a life that is grounded on freedom and comfort—nothing extravagant. To that extent, learning is a means to an end.

Now, considering that there's a category of content that students can't accurately diagnose the utility of, why then do they resort to a utilitarian rationale? I would argue that they do this out of frustration, not out of the belief that everything in school must make sense through their own eyes. Kids aren't stupid. The conceptual value of school is not lost on them. So, if a class is taught by teachers that aren't enthusiastic about the material, if teachers aren't enjoying *themselves*, or if a class is taught without emphasizing the beauty, awe and wonder of the knowledge being imparted, is there any purpose of investing valuable time and energy into the class? Simply for the grade?

Well, we all know that passing can be achieved without learning, so why try? As a result, students resort to questioning the utility of it in the working world.

And yes, all subjects taught in school have beauty, awe and wonder deeply ingrained in them. There is no debate here. Just think about it. Math, Science, Language, History, to name a few, are all literally the truths of our universe. They represent the sum total of all that has been achieved by the human race, by us. It's the culmination of many millennia of energy spent by our own species, and genetically speaking, by the students themselves. There is nothing more beautiful and inspiring than that. It may not be something to pursue indefinitely, but even a rudimentary understanding of these concepts broadens horizons to a degree impossible by any other means.

When I connected these dots, my eyes were opened to a very cold harsh truth that I, and countless others, have been victims of—that school has the potential to be exceptionally fun. When else does one, free from any responsibility, get the opportunity to learn the truths of the universe and nothing else? And yet, school sucks. It feels like being stuck in the middle of an endless traffic jam. There is no escape except through endurance.

And to drive home the claim that only as a last resort do children rationalize not learning by questioning its utility—think about sports, video games or food! What is the point of eating different cuisines if all that is needed is the satiation of hunger? What is the point of playing a video game if it's not going to help you land a better job? What's the point of playing a sport if exercise is all you need? The answer to all are the same—because you enjoy it! Now, a natural response to that may be, 'But I don't enjoy learning'. Fair enough, but recognize that if learning was not something you were biologically wired to do, your genetic makeup would not have made it this far. As for the absence of pleasure, here is where we come back to the teacher. It's their job to make it pleasurable! Especially in today's day and age. And when the majority fail to do so, we naturally fall back on the utilitarian rationale of education, which is, 'I am going to school—something that's not fun—to get into college/a job.'

The next problem comes in the form of many teachers being unable to think from different perspectives. There is no *one* way to learn. What happens in the classroom is that teachers default to communicating through the lens of how they learned, oblivious to the countless other paths through which the student may attain the same understanding. It all becomes very circular. The teacher explains a concept, students don't understand it, the teacher attempts to explain it again with different words, students still don't understand, and then either time-constraints force the teacher to move on, or the students say they understand, even though they don't. It's not as if the teacher doesn't *try* to explain it in a way that the student can understand, it's just that it takes *a lot* of skill and experience to do so. In essence, these teachers are victims of the curse of knowledge. They lost their ability to view the material they teach through the lens of a student.

And then we have a group of teachers that are criminally ignored. Those who should, and hopefully will, be replaced by robots as soon as possible! All they do is repeat textbook material, and sometimes, word-for-word! If you're lucky, they might add in a PowerPoint presentation. But the end result is the same—regurgitation of a textbook that, ironically, had to be purchased for the class in the first place. This is especially true in higher education. We are spending thousands of dollars for the narration of a text that we could just read on our own, at a fraction of the cost. A good teacher talks *with* someone, not *at* someone. This is 101 stuff. Teaching is conversational, it involves organic reciprocity; it must flow like water. That's how one can ensure that students are actively engaged and not just alternating between passive consumption and complete ignorance of the material being taught.

It's also important to note that the teachers aren't solely at fault; many are dependent on the current landscape of the education system. If they don't adhere to the external pressures imposed, they may very well lose their livelihood. For example, when all that is allotted is an hour, how can one expect to address each unique issue a class of twenty/thirty students may have?

Impossible.

It's honestly a depressing sight; teachers are aware of this drawback and are helpless. Over the years, many have come to accept students slipping through the cracks as an inevitability. In higher education specifically, with the priority being top-line growth, professors are forced into the situation of teaching an ever-increasing number of heads in spite of experiencing drops in learning quality first-hand. To add to that, the shift to hiring a predominantly adjunct professoriate has discouraged many to prioritize student learning as their time horizon at any given school is shortened; learning can only happen with large time and energy investments. And lastly, like I've touched upon already, tenure actively discourages the quality of teaching to meet standards. In fact, many tenured professors, especially those at large research universities, not only perceive teaching as a waste of time but also were never hired for their ability to teach in the first place. They were hired to conduct research and only accepted teaching as an inevitable drawback of the job.

At the end of the day, it's a supply problem. Being a good teacher is no easy task. Consequently, the immense difficulty of the profession makes the supply sparse rather naturally, whereas the demand is only limited to the population of our species. However, there is good news. Given the maturation of the internet, it is not the tools to learn that are lacking. As Naval Ravikant succinctly said, 'The means to learn are abundant. It is the desire to learn that is scarce.' This implies a transformation in what it means to be a teacher. To facilitate this desire, to challenge, and to guide the social process of learning—this is what a teacher is, not simply a source of data transfer.

No Mastery Learning

What is Mastery Learning? Well, it's the solution to all our problems! Okay, maybe that's classic premature optimism. Nevertheless, it's definitely our ticket to the next big leap in learning outcomes if ever there was one.

In a nutshell, it's a pedagogical philosophy that says that a student should progress into a more advanced level of study *only* when he has acquired an adequate comprehension of the current level. It sounds simple, but one should not turn a deaf ear to its significance.

Let me emphasize the idea. In the traditional model, time is fixed and learning outcomes are variable—a year per grade, and anything above around 70 per cent is considered a passing grade. In Mastery Learning, the entire model is flipped. The learning outcome is fixed, while the time is rendered variable. Sure, some students might grasp a particular subject faster than the others, but at the end of the day, they all reach the same level of comprehension that is necessary to grasp the topic.

I was first introduced to this by Salman Khan of Khan Academy, but was surprised to learn that this model had been introduced a long time ago.

In 1919, American educator Charleton Washburne, became the head of an affluent school in Chicago, USA. Three-years later, he introduced a radical idea, going against what was considered *the right way of doing things*. It consisted of two core pillars: (1) The belief that all students can attain a thorough understanding of any concept, given the appropriate conditions. (2) Structuring the curriculum based on target levels of comprehension rather than time.

Unsurprisingly—in hindsight, that is—it was a huge success! Mysteriously, even though Washburne ended up serving as president of the Progressive Education Association, his ideas gradually faded into oblivion. Well, not *so* mysteriously. You see, this model was expensive. It needed not only rigorous teacher-retraining but also a whole host of supplemental material and equipment. It's important to remember that after the first World War, American economy was thriving, which was partly why this educational experiment was even conducted. But soon, the costs associated with scaling nationwide, coupled with the skyrocketing costs of the imminent WW2 climate, made it incredibly unsustainable.

For almost four decades this educational model endured ignorance, and was finally resurrected in the 1960s by developmental psychologist, Benjamin Bloom and his protégé, James Block.[1] Their philosophy was essentially the same as Washburne's and so, it was rolled out to various schools all over the country. Once again, it was a huge success. Studies after studies proved the efficacy of the system. One concluded that,

> Students in mastery learning programs at all levels showed increased gains in achievement over those in traditional instruction programs…Students retained what they had learned longer under mastery learning, both in short-term and long-term studies.[2]

Another concluded,

> Mastery learning reduces the academic spread between the slower and faster students without slowing down the faster students.[3]

Further still, another found that,

> Teachers who [used] mastery learning…began to feel better about teaching and their roles as teachers.[4]

Everything seemed to be pointing in one direction! Unfortunately, in spite of the clarity of findings, this system once again faded into obscurity. This time the reason for it was more of an enigma. The cost element still played a role, but there certainly weren't external factors suppressing mainstream adoption to the same degree. Nonetheless, this time around, one thing was made clear—it wasn't *only* economic factors that stagnated its adoption. The inertia of the status quo actively resisted this radical change. The people in power, naturally, resented change if it meant displacement. So, any and all arguments opposing the concept were exploited.

And this brings us to today.

Using the technology available, the cost to implement this model has been driven to an all-time low, while demand for education reform is on the rise—and rightfully so! There's a whole host of anti-learning phenomena our time-based system promotes. Generations of students have been systematically deprived of the opportunity to fulfil their true potential. I say this not with a tone of righteous indignation but that of disappointment; the issues are blatantly evident. We either don't bother to look, or have come to accept the way it is. I, for one, think that's lazy and downright evil. So, as the natural first step, I shall lay out all that is grossly nefarious about the system we subject our youth to.

∽

The belief in the fixed *one revolution around the sun per level of study* is the core assumption underpinning the whole system. Almost all the drawbacks I will touch upon are mere consequences of this.

The first implication is obvious—a time-based philosophy implemented in the macro naturally results in a time-based philosophy in the micro. In other words, the lecture. The imposition of X minutes of class time per body of knowledge. Irony is, it ignores very prominent research on how students actually learn.

∽

- A meta-analysis consisted of 225 unique studies that compared lectures to active learning seminars. One of the many findings was that the lecture model of education led to 55 per cent of failures at student learning, relative to the active learning seminar.[5]
- A 1969 study showed students recalled less than 20 per cent of a lecture even three-days later.[6]
- A more recent study, in 2000, showed students recalled less than 10 per cent of a lecture after three-days.[7]
- In 1996, there was a finding published in the National Teaching & Learning Forum regarding students' focus during a typical class period. It showed that students would need 3-5 minutes to settle down, followed by 10-18 minutes of optimal focus and then, a lapse in attention. Optimal focus would definitely return, but as this pattern went on, it would always return in incrementally smaller chunks. By the end of the class, the optimal focus block fell to 3-4 minutes only![8]
- Another study tested students' recollection of material from a twenty-minute presentation broken into four segments of five-minutes, with the hypothesis that the last segment would be the one most memorable. However, the results showed the complete opposite. Students remembered most content from the first five-minutes! By the fifteen-minute mark, they'd completely zoned out.[9] A scary thought is that both these findings were made before the age of the internet and social media. For all we know, attention spans have been falling further while the quantity of lecture time has been skyrocketing.

∽

In all honesty, while students sit at desks painstakingly trying to consume information, anything from an infinite array of possibilities can be a cause for distraction. A fight with a friend, feeling unwell, the concept being taught already understood, thinking about a crush, cramming for another class, family matters, still trying to figure out the preceding topic—the list goes on. As a result, at any given moment, the majority of a class is either lost or bored, while only a minority is following along. And once the lecture is over, the topic isn't coming back! The teacher must move to the next if she is to complete the syllabus on time.

Another factor (this point may seem moot and, frankly speaking, stupid, but I assure you it's not) that makes the in-class lecture ineffective is the face. Let me explain. Even though teaching should be an intimate experience, faces can be a very powerful source of distraction. Blinking eyes, a moving mouth, twitchy eyebrows, and all the other peculiar characteristics of humans. Everyone has experienced being distracted in conversation due to this, and the same applies to learning.

A great example is what's known as *reflexive gaze following*. When we glance into someone's eyes, ours automatically orient themselves on the same spot theirs is directed at. We believe this reflex emerged to aid us in comprehending what someone else is thinking or trying to communicate before the maturation of complex language. And we see it in children as young as six months old![10] So, when teachers inevitably make their way around the classroom, it subconsciously causes students to follow the teacher's line of sight, which inadvertently distracts from the material at hand.

Now, this doesn't mean we shouldn't have face-to-face interaction. Of course we should, that's what makes learning a social activity. However, like with anything, there's a time and place for it. The best opportunity for it would be *after* a student has been acquainted with the subject. When a student is being exposed to new material, all that they should be focusing on is the concept. A better process would be one in which a student first learns from a faceless online video at home, followed by face-to-face discussions in the classroom. In fact, following this process, due to the extra time freed up in the classroom, the teacher becomes a more potent force.

One way people recommend tackling the lecture's evident drawbacks is by reducing the number of students. Unfortunately, this is akin to using a bandage for a bullet wound. Obviously, fewer students in a class allows for more personal relationships to develop, but to think this alone will stop students from falling behind is naive.

This is because people have different speeds of learning based on the nature of the material presented. For any given subject, some may intuitively grasp the concepts, while others may have to go through the trenches. Interestingly, the student who intuitively catches on to a topic may very well find themselves struggling with another topic within the same subject. A good example of this is mathematics; while rationality and attention to detail are needed in basic arithmetic, abstract creativity is the driving force in topics like complex/imaginary numbers. Also, *picking up faster* is neither a guaranteed positive nor an accurate measure of intelligence; seldom does it equate to deep understanding. As Mr Khan says,

> The tortoise may very well end up with more knowledge—more useful, lasting knowledge—than the hare.[11]

Authority figures are quick to respond with constant affirmations— 'Feel free to ask questions' or 'No question is a bad question.' This is all fine and dandy, but it ignores two important truths. We are social beings and education is a social activity. To disregard the ever-present social implications is daft. Nobody in their right mind would argue that peer pressure is not a powerful force, so why do we forget it exists when we enter the classrooms? What I'm getting at is the repetition of the same question being posed to the teacher, over and over again, and the audible increase in frustration in the teacher's tone. The consequence of holding up the entire class for a doubt that pertains to only a single individual is one of the most common reasons why students avoid asking questions, and sacrifice learning in the process.

And the issue flows both ways. When teachers with good intentions ask questions, correct answers are expected immediately. This causes thought-paralysis. With the fear of getting the answer incorrect, the student wants neither judgement from their peers nor to disappoint the teacher.

At the end of the day, there will always be inconsistency in learning, regardless of the student-teacher ratio. Even if a class consists of exactly one student and one teacher, there is no guarantee that learning will be effective if the class has to be carried out at a predetermined pace. Suffice to say, when the time comes to take the test, a significant number of students remain with an inadequate level of comprehension *in spite* of attending every single class. Chances are, they would have *eventually* gotten it. But the system isn't designed for an eventual understanding—the show must go on.

So, if research and everyday empirical findings clearly show the flaws of the lecture format, why the hell is it the dominant form of teaching? Well, one reason is the logistical ease. It's never been a good system for the learner, only for the teacher. When observed through the lens of administration and faculty, there simply isn't a system which is as scalable and efficient as the lecture. The effort needed to lecture one, ten or a hundred students is essentially the same. This, then, becomes a consequence of the fact that all learning is restricted by time.

Moving on to the *emphasis on 'subjects'*.

Let us take a moment to recollect why this exists in the first place. In a world where menial labor was the prerequisite for national growth, the ability to *connect the dots*, to *think big*, was a detriment. A worker had to do what they were told, and that was it. Through this lens, the artificial division of intricately intertwined bodies of knowledge was a positive. However, today, it paints a very misleading and disjointed view of the world to our youth. The world is not black and white. There is no good and bad. The world is a complex system and for years on end, we subliminally tell students the exact opposite.

A stereotypical day in school constitutes a sequence of classes, each receiving a fixed amount of time to disseminate information. Neither is there any communication between teachers nor a willingness to design curricula to emphasize relationships between content. Knowledge is siloed; and in silos it remains in the student's mind. It's embarrassing, but it took me almost two decades to realize that biology is nothing but, quite literally, big chemistry. Chemistry is nothing but big physics. Most embarrassing of all, science is nothing but evolved philosophy. This seems obvious in hindsight, but I would put money on the majority of high school students being oblivious to the linkages between philosophy and science.

Further still, each subject is chopped up and thrown at us, as if each have their own place in the world. They call it *units*. Now, within the main silo, we have sub-silos. The ringing of the bell marks the time to stop thinking about a subject; moving on to the next unit is a green light to stop thinking about the preceding one. This unitization happens in every subject—content is taught, tested and then we move to the next. The previous topic is now finished, even though, in reality, no material is *ever finished*. Knowledge is not static but a dynamic flow of ideas. Even Sir Isaac Newton's research—ideas that stood unchanged for over 200 years—evolved with a little helping hand from Einstein.

A natural consequence of this is the dissemination of material in parallel. What I refer to here is the compulsion of learning different subjects simultaneously. Unlike what much of the modern education system might promote, multi-tasking is an evil when it comes to learning. Not in the stereotypical sense of the word (that's a conversation for another day), but the pedagogy of teaching several subjects within any given period of time. For true learning to take place, one's mind must be fully immersed in the material being taught for a sustained period, without any distractions. One must surround themselves with what they intend to learn, and only over time will it be absorbed. Learning is like marination, it is useless if it isn't given adequate time and exposure.

Building on this, a bigger problem is neither that too much is taught nor that it is done so simultaneously, but that knowledge is disseminated in their own discrete contexts. Like I mentioned, the world is interconnected in many ways, and if multiple subjects are to be taught, it must be done with relationships clearly defined. Here's why.

Our memory can be divided into two categories—short- and long-term. Short-term (ST) memory is fragile and fleeting, whereas long-term (LT) memory is stable and durable. All information is first retained as ST memory, and only then does it have the chance of being retained as LT memory. Now, the mechanism through which ST memory becomes LT memory is known as *consolidation*. And, as neuroscientist Eric Kandel writes:

> This is accomplished by attending to the information and associating it meaningfully and systematically with knowledge already well established in memory.[12]

This is known as *Associative Learning*, and can be defined as the process by which a deeper comprehension and more durable memory is achieved through relating something new to something already known. Think of it as pattern recognition.

Your brain is an inconceivably complex network of billions of neurons, each interconnected in trillions of possible ways. Every new thought is a physical alteration within this network. Critically, your thoughts are a direct product of the information consumed, which is nothing but what hits the senses. In other words, every time something is seen, heard, touched, felt or smelled, it is information being absorbed. This means that the brain has a perpetual *information overload* problem. To solve this problem, the brain uses patterns.

Kevin Carrey explains it well:

Consider the sentence 'My mother bought an encyclopedia'. When you read the word 'encyclopedia', it required very little time and mental effort for you to understand what it meant. You did not consider the shape of each letter in turn, as a small child might, carefully relating each to a specific sound and then linking them together to form a word: 'en-sigh-klo-pee-dee-ah.' That's because before you read that sentence, a pattern had already been created in your brain, involving a specific set of neurons linked together by axons, dendrites, and synapses, representing the word 'encyclopedia'... you have spent thousands of hours reading over years of your life, that pattern is very well established, and the connections between the neurons are quite strong. So your brain required only a brief glance at that combination of letters to understand that it meant 'encyclopedia' and all the word implies. The process was largely automatic...the brain's capacity for pattern recognition is adaptable, flexible, and strong. If the word in that sentence had been spelled 'encylopedia,' you would not have been utterly baffled, even though it is missing the second letter c. You might not have even noticed the mistake at all.[13]

This is no fad. In 1973, a study of human memory was published by Herbert Simon and William Chase. They invited chess players—ranging from beginners to grandmasters—and showed each a chessboard with pieces randomly arranged for five seconds. The task was to recollect their position from memory. All, on average, could remember about four correct positions only. Subsequently, the exercise was repeated; however, this time the piece positions concurred with the rules of the game. Now, the veterans significantly outperformed the rookies. Why? Two words—associative learning. The players with years of experience had neural patterns built for where each piece could be positioned.[14,15]

To really drive home the point, try the following activity (adopted from the book *Made to Stick*).[16] Here's what you do: Glance over the letters, close the book and then note down as many letters as you can remember. Only after doing so, turn the page.

I MFFB IUN ES CON ASAU SSRW HO

Now repeat the exercise. The rules are the same. The only difference is that the letters have been re-arranged. Same letters, different sequence.

IMF FBI UNESCO NASA USSR WHO

My guess is you performed better this time.

Why? Associative memory. You aren't using rote this time around, you already have many associations in your brain corresponding to these letters.

Bottom line, the best way to teach material is by making the flow of content as explicit as possible. Still, it doesn't happen. Knowing all this, can we really blame students for forgetting almost everything they studied right after the exam? They were neither given a reason to remember the content, nor was it presented in a way that facilitated deep comprehension.

Another phenomenon that time-based learning demands is *the overvaluation of tests*. As a concept, I see its value. It definetly justifies a place in the system. Unfortunately, that place is most definitely not where it's at today. For the greater part of a decade, our model of education relies on tests as gateways to progress. We are explicitly telling students that, 'as long as you pass the test, you will succeed'. This is criminal. Because the logical flipside to that assertion is, 'If you can't pass, you won't succeed'. And this mentality sticks with students, in some cases—lifelong. For a pretty faulty tool, this is quite a sad outcome.

I say faulty because tests, for all their worth, are pretty worthless when it comes to many factors that determine success. For one, it provides a purely historic picture of a student. It's nothing but a snapshot of a student at a moment in time. And considering people learn at different rates, it makes it all the more dubious. We learn zilch about the student's potential to learn, information retained post-test, rationale behind the student achieving the score (for example, was it rote memorization? Cheating? A lapse in attention? Lack of time? A sound understanding?), or if the student learned the material in its entirety! This last point is comically true. It's a well-known fact that tests are based on a subset of the study material, therefore, it could've been dumb luck that the content studied just so happened to be on the test, while the exact opposite could've been the downfall of another student.

As Mr Khan puts it,

> Tests measure the approximate state of a student's memory and perhaps understanding, in regard to a particular subset of subject matter at a given moment in time, it being understood that the measurement can vary considerably and randomly according to the particular questions being asked.[17]

When put like that, it's quite astounding that entire lives rest on such weak shoulders. At best, a good test—note that I said good—is a measure of a student's preparedness, not their potential.

In culmination of my case against testing, I want to leave you with an excerpt from Peter Grey's *Free to Learn*.

> Parents, teachers, schools and whole school districts—not just the child—are evaluated these days on the basis of children's test performance. Children are pawns in a competitive game in which the adults around them are trying to squeeze the highest possible scores out of them on standardized tests. Anything that increases performance short of outright cheating is considered 'education' in this high-stakes game. Thus, drills that enhance short-term memory of information they will be tested on are considered legitimate education, even though such drills produce no increase at all in understanding.[18]

Test-based grading, too, contains its own set of obstacles, further hindering students' capacity to learn. We need only to look back to the reason why grading became a staple. In a world where extreme social mobility was seen as burdensome to the nation, there was a

Salman Khan of Khan Academy

"Tests measure the approximate state of a student's memory and perhaps understanding, in regard to a particular subset of subject matter at a given moment in time, it being understood that the measurement can vary considerably and randomly according to the particular questions being asked."

need for a system which, at least on the surface, seemed scientific and fair. We needed the majority of the labour supply to do mundane, repetitive work and what better way to provide the illusion of a fair shot than by creating a tangible rationale, in the form of a grade, to funnel masses into the workforce?

This isn't a dystopian view of the past. Just think back to the percentage of students in your schooling days that were straight A's; chances are, they were a small minority. The situation was the same back then! The majority of students who didn't display 'extraordinary intelligence' would be satisfied by a career of mind-numbing work, after all, their grade 'proved' they weren't cut out for higher-level positions. On the surface, it was a win for all parties involved.

Times have changed. Grading is outdated. Employers are demanding the opposite—mundane, repetitive work has transformed into critical thinking, creative thinking, ability to identify second-order consequences, etc. Grades, however, continue to perform the same task for which they were originally intended; students still believe the grade is the all-important factor that determines one's prospects. To the smallest of degrees, it may be true, but life is a marathon, and no marathon has ever been won by focusing on the sprint while ignoring endurance.

In other words, when grades are seen as the end game, learning becomes an unnecessary hurdle that returns very little for the enormous time and energy it demands. Given these conditions, students will always do the bare minimum needed to achieve the highest possible score. Grades reduce the value of learning, discouraging one from developing their ability to learn, which is the real all-important factor that determines life prospects.

Subsequently, in the collective's push to attain higher grades, curriculum tends to morph into test preparation. Instead of a curriculum design based on what should be learned, we base it on how to get the maximum score. And, as a third-order consequence, grades tend to get inflated.[19] It's a well-known fact that problems arise when incentives are not aligned—education is no different. Even though institutions exist to promote learning, the reality is that each student who fails is a negative reflection on the teacher and the institution. In higher education, this problem is compounded; a professor's job is tied to student evaluations, incentivizing them to not only sacrifice learning outcomes but also make tests easier in an attempt to receive positive reviews from the broadest student base. Murray Sperber, a higher education analyst, refers to it as a 'non-aggression pact'.[20] And, as covered before, learning amongst students is never prioritized, so standards organically reduce if mass flunking is to be avoided. All this inevitably leads to the incremental increase in not only grades received (despite falling learning standards), but also the discrepancy between the value of each grade across institutions. In fact, many employers don't even look at applicants' grades as they know it seldom predicts good job performance. One company, Google, found almost no correlation between the two, so it stopped asking.[21]

Like I've said, I don't recommend throwing the baby out with the bathwater. Test-based grading definitely provides some valuable information and should rightfully be utilized. However, adaptation and optimization is required if the needs of a wider group of students are to be catered to. Even more so as the next unintended consequence discussed is much more subtle.

More often than we like to admit, grades act as self-fulfilling prophecies. In other words, when students are labeled as 'B' or 'C' students, they themselves start believing that's who they naturally are. Thus, a false belief is reinforced; the thought itself is a cause for it to actually become true. A famous example of the effect of such labels took place in 1968.

The day after MLK was assassinated, an elementary school teacher, Jane Elliott, tried to explain to a confused class of third-graders why anyone would want Dr King dead.

She recollected, 'I knew it was time to deal with this in a concrete way, because we'd talked about discrimination since the first day of school. But the shooting... couldn't be explained to little third-graders in Riceville, Iowa.' Her solution was genius. The next day, she divided the class into two: brown-eyed and blue-eyed kids. And proceeded with the announcement that, 'They're [the blue-eyed kids] the better people in the room'. The rest were made to wear collars. Elliott recounts her observation, 'I watched those kids turn into nasty, vicious, discriminating third-graders…friendships seemed to dissolve instantly…it was ghastly'.

The next day, she began the class with the announcement that she was wrong; it was the brown-eyed who were superior. Still, discrimination persisted, but the direction flipped. Most important to our context is the effect it had on their academic performance. On the first day, the brown-eyed kids took 5.5 minutes to go through the reading exercises, on the next day (when they were labelled 'superior'), only 2.5 minutes. When Elliot asked the brown-eyed kids, 'Why couldn't you go this fast yesterday?' Their response was, 'We had those collars on' and, 'We couldn't stop thinking about those collars.'[22]

Although this exercise was done to explain prejudices and discrimination, it sheds light on how applying labels creates *looping effects*. The label changes one's behaviour, becoming a self-fulfilling prophecy.[23] Grades tend to work the same way. It rigidly defines who students are, disincentivizing effort to change. Expectations drop and willingness to improve drops with it. Then, this label goes on to be a deciding factor—often as a limiting agent—for the path they choose in life.

Bringing me to my next point, *tracking*.

As students trot along in the system, a time comes when a student must figure out if they are one of the 'intelligent', 'average' or 'slow' students. This decision dictates the information they will be exposed to in the future.

We are told that this is to allow the student to work with material of their level. On the surface, this makes sense. In reality, it's not only another consequence of the time-based model, but also attractive to administrators due to its convenient facilitation by test-based grades.

I get it, tracking students is logistically easier than having a class full of many students, each at separate levels of understanding. This makes sense at first glance, but a moment's critical thought exposes its laziness. In the world of software engineering, there's a term called *technical debt*. Derived from regular debt (used in finance), it is a future cost to be paid, often at a surplus to the principal. Similarly, technical debt is a measure of future work to be done as a consequence of choosing an easy but limited solution now, over a more robust but time-consuming approach. I argue that tracking is only needed when we accumulate *educational debt.* In other words, when our ineffective pedagogy, over many years, results in widening gaps in student learning, time constraints force us to eventually track students as the resources required to fill the gaps become too great. Now, tracking becomes a necessity, and a dangerous one at that.

See, when we are bound by time, we are forced to make decisions based only on the information at hand, not on its accuracy or reliability. This holds true for every aspect of life. I say this because having established how truly atrocious tests are at providing data on future potential, it seems odd that they would be used to determine exactly that. If I haven't made it clear already, students learn at different rates based on the nature of material, how it is presented and their engagement/ interest. So, when we track students, what we're effectively doing is determining a student's future based on *their current ability to attain a quick understanding of a subset of the subject material.* For all we know, a student who takes five times longer to grasp the foundational material than the stereotypical best student may be a source of great insight into the same field of knowledge down the line. But we nip it in the bud.

Don't believe me? The Khan Academy software has been keeping track of student-progress over time in a mastery learning environment. And the data clearly indicates that students who are bang-average halfway through a period of time, can and do end up on top later.[24] Within our system of tracking, chances are that they would've been boxed in the 'average' batch and not seen their potential realized.

Additional to emphasizing the self-fulfilling prophecy of the grade, tracking also suppresses creativity. Schools routinely talk about the value of creativity, but their actions paint a different picture. This is for two reasons.

1. By tracking, we restrict creative development by pushing students away from its catalysts. When students are labeled as slow, they're slotted into the lower classes, which come with inferior teachers, more mundane material and even lower expectations. Inadvertently, we end up discouraging students whose talents are of a different nature—the late bloomers, the ones that think differently. There are two types of knowledge: (1) A type with an ambiguous character that is defined by its inability to be put into a box and labelled. It cannot be grasped in a linear fashion from the ground up. Sometimes it emerges after consistent execution of tried-and-tested methodology over a long period of time, sometimes by trial and error and sometimes, by dumb-luck. (2) The type that exists in binary— right or wrong. Thus, it provides convenient identification and can be subject to timely diagnosis of labels and grades. Problem is, even though both hold immense value, school only values the second. When we test with the intention of filtration—and that's what tracking really is—we abort creativity.

2. Creativity simply can't be tested for. All our tests are based on prerequisite elements and base necessities. For example, to track students in math or science, most of what we test is theory and application of formula. This is like testing a

musician on her ability to read musical notations, a writer on his knowledge of grammar and vocabulary or a painter on her knowledge of shapes and colours. Sure, these abilities help, but it says nothing about their potential to manifest a true creative end-product.

Once again, Mr Khan said it perfectly,

> The skills and knowledge that tests can measure are merely warm-up exercises.[25]

And this philosophy of only testing prerequisite material ties back to one of the core issues of K-12—their prestige derived from college placements, which is only in the short term. Creativity isn't something that just shows up at your beck and call, it's almost always a long-term investment.

Bringing me to my last point—*negligence of the mixed-age classrooms.*

When this is all that we have known, age-based cohorts makes sense. They have set expectations, curriculum is designed accordingly, information is disseminated by lecture, tests follow and based on their result, the student moves on to the next set of expectations. It all seems structured, advanced, purposeful, systematized…scientific! Best of all, it's rather convenient to execute! It just *works*.

Unfortunately, age-based grouping is one of the worst consequences of our educational model. Like subjects, units and class periods, it's just another way knowledge has been divided up, to provide an idea different from the truth; another outdated fiction made by us, neither inevitable nor ideal.

Importantly, age-based restriction is not how humans work; it's not how our species has learned for 99 per cent of our existence.[26] No hunter-gatherers, or even someone today, has ever said, 'Yeah, I don't mind having two kids but only if they're twins, otherwise their learning will be sub-optimal.' Going back even further, age-mixing among the young was the norm. Our great ape relatives—chimpanzees, bonobos, gorillas—all live in small social groups where females reproduce one at a time, making interaction between youngsters of different ages inevitable.[27] This gives us insight into where our play and learning instincts have evolved from. To not utilize it to our advantage would be like using a dictionary when Siri and Alexa are a phrase away.

To be honest, I don't think anyone would deny the observation that children benefit from growing up amongst people of different ages. But, for the sake of our learning institutions, let me break it down nonetheless.

What are the benefits for the young?

Well, first, it allows them to indulge in activities that are in their *zone of proximal development*. In the 1930s, Russian psychologist Lev Vygotsky coined this term to refer to activities a child cannot do alone or with others of the same ability, but can do in collaboration with others who are more skilled.[28] This idea was further extrapolated by Harvard psychologist, Jerome Bruner and his team, with the introduction of the term *scaffolding*—a metaphor that describe the means through which skilled participants facilitate novices to engage in shared activities.[29] In other words, an older or more skilled participant engages the younger in the zone of proximal development by erecting scaffolds. For example, if two brothers—six and twelve years of age—play catch, the older brother will intentionally throw the ball at a velocity and angle at which the younger one must work hard to catch it, but is yet within his reach.

The same applies to mental games. In fact, research shows that this method leads to a quicker acquisition of skills like reading, writing and arithmetic. For example, in a study where four to ten-year-olds at a summer program were videotaped playing freely, one instance in a role-playing game showed an older child explaining to a younger one how much it would cost to buy certain items, how much change he would receive, etc. This sounds rudimentary, but we must remember that such concepts make a lot more sense to children when they have a firm grasp on the context (in this case the game), as they can explicitly relate to the new concept being learned; unlike in the more abstract and involuntary instance of the classroom.[30]

Second, we have learning by observation. This is as instinctive as education gets. Kids observe how elders conduct themselves, which then gives them ideas as to how things are done (and some are even inspired in the process). Interestingly, scaffolding happens indirectly here as well. For example, by listening to more sophisticated language, younger ones tend to expand their own vocabulary and thought-processes. Also, it's important to note that children often tend to mimic those who are slightly older as opposed to adults. To the six-year-old, adults are a completely different species well out of reach, but the cool ten-year-old? Well, that's someone they can aspire to be. This is how learning occurs naturally. Each age-group tends to mimic the age-group that's incrementally older. No one needs to establish themselves as role models, they automatically are.

And last, but not least, learning is facilitated by a sense of safety and emotional support. This point is relatively straightforward. Not to say that traditional schooling doesn't actively promote a safe and nurturing environment, but the model used today is limited by numbers—there's only one authority figure, only one person who can help. Resulting in some students feeling isolated, lost, and all the negative emotions that arise once one proceeds further down this path. Whereas, in a multi-age classroom, it's impossible to not be heard or find guidance! It's almost a guarantee that an older child will aid a younger one, even if they don't have to. It's like a hack—the existence of the young student triggers nurturing instincts in the older fellows, making them feel compelled to help.[31]

And this brings me to the next section—the benefits of mixed-age play for older students.

Following from the last point, on the flip side, older kids gain the opportunity to mature. Precisely by helping those in need, they practice leadership, nurturance and responsibility in a relationship. Take this away and not only do the young lose role models but the old lose an opportunity to develop critical skills. This is no trivial matter. Today, there is a seemingly endless outcry regarding teenage behaviour. Apathy, mental health issues, suicide—the list goes on. I acknowledge that these are complex issues but a cause of this, no doubt, is our avoidance, and explicit skepticism, to entrust them with real responsibility; responsibility not that of handling themselves, but that of which if they don't fulfil, *another* life may be affected. By restricting students to interact with the same age cohort, we only enforce responsibility for themselves—keep in mind, a defining characteristic of being an adult is responsibility that goes beyond oneself. Ultimately, we infantilize them, and infants they tend to remain.

Most of all, we expect kids to take control of their lives. Yes, it's a very broad and abstract concept to instill, but a great way to do this is, as Dr Peterson asserts, to treat yourself like someone you're responsible for helping. This maxim is one that is easy to remember and facilitates fruitful decision making. But, if you are to treat yourself like someone you are responsible for, you must first know *how* to help someone; and that, is a natural consequence of the mixed-age classroom.

This next point is one that I, too, can attest—learning through teaching. This practice is known as the *Feynman technique* and, time-after-time, it has proven to be a potent tool.

In the traditional school model, the existence of a single teacher tends to result in students having to wait their turn for the teacher's attention. In a mixed-age classroom, however, the older kids can step in to solve this problem while benefiting simultaneously. This is because it forces the student-teachers to think deeply about knowledge that's at the edge of their comprehension. Often, the learner considers the concept from angles the older student hadn't thought of before, making the concept clearer. Here lies a truth that applies to all—the act of teaching and learning is a bidirectional activity. Both have

A mixed classroom

something to take from it. In my experience, some teachers display this understanding but many seldom acknowledge it.

Wrapping this section up, children on both sides of the age spectrum have something to gain, and both rise to the occasion. The mixed-age classroom model solves a great number of problems simultaneously. Namely, it reduces the heavy burden of teaching from the teacher, discourages bullying, compels older students to revise past topics and allows those who are of equal ability, regardless of age, to form community. Considering we're in the twenty-first century, it truly is an enigma why we don't conduct class in this manner.

∽

With that, we come to the end of my rant against the individual parts that make traditional schooling a detriment rather than a benefit to student learning. However, the crucial takeaway from this section shouldn't be the cogs in the machine but the implication of the entire system working in unison. Why do some students clearly outperform the rest while others seem like a lost cause? Is it just the way it is? Some are blessed, others aren't? Maybe, but definitely not to the degree we see on a grade distribution.

As I lightly touched upon earlier, the time-based model tends to not only cause large knowledge gaps in student learning, but also leave them unaddressed. Over time, these gaps turn into taxing obstacles, and eventually, the obstacles turn into impassable roadblocks. Think about it like building a house. Would we begin construction with a foundation that is anything less than a hundred percent acceptable? I hope not. But let's say we did, and with every layer we did the same. What will happen? Eventually, the whole thing will come crashing down![32] The same applies to learning. It's not rocket science.

And it's not that this concept is new and unfamiliar. In martial arts, we aren't allowed to proceed to the next belt until we master the current; similarly when learning music. But when it comes to traditional schooling, we let kids pass even if they don't have a firm grasp on the subject. We tell ourselves it's the right thing to do, when in reality, we're just postponing their eventual demise. Without a solid grasp of letters, how can anyone be expected to understand words? And yet the teacher continues the lecture on sentences.

This is also why a vast majority of students can't seem to relate material they have learned to outside the classroom. For any concept 'learned', only a superficial understanding ever made its way into existence. By design we memorize it with the intention—no, the pleasure—of forgetting it later. Back in middle school, I vividly remember routinely questioning the utility of mathematics. Out of all the subjects, it was mathematics that I couldn't see value in! How could one be so shortsighted to not see the value of a field so explicitly present in every walk of life?

In hindsight, the answer is obvious. Not once did I develop a deep comprehension of any concept. And this is the truth for most students in countries all over the world—superficial knowledge of a lot, mastery of none.

But hold on—if the gaps are the issue, wouldn't it be easier to fill them rather than revamp an entire system?

In theory, maybe. But in practice, who would do it? School definitely won't. It would take days, weeks, maybe months! We can't address each student on a case-by-case basis—we'll have to sacrifice the next unit! Another option, then, is to seek aid outside the school. Private tutors? This can get very expensive very fast, not to mention the incremental time it requires as well.

The last option would be for the student to figure it out themselves. This is not only easier said than done but also incredibly hypocritical and unfair. School, since the beginning, has taught us to be passive beings that absorb information to be regurgitated when the time comes. Now, suddenly, we're expected to not only transform into the polar opposite by being proactive, but also self-diagnose years of setbacks?! The habit of passivity is an incredibly hard one to break out of, especially for brains lacking the maturation of the prefrontal cortex.

To be fair, we're given a glimpse of opportunity in college. Meeting a professor outside of the classroom or during designated office hours definitely helps. But other than the additional time cost incurred, what if the student has other obligations? Other class work? What if the student, after more than a decade of traditional schooling, has developed a deep cynicism towards the institution of learning? To impose an arbitrary education system on students, and further frame it as their responsibility, is a model that produces an illusion of equal opportunity. And, simultaneously, takes on the task of student learning with unnecessary friction, in spite of there being plenty of research affirming the fact that it doesn't need to be this way.

In conclusion, structurally, the current education system's core competency is identification. It excels at categorizing students as they are now—not their potential—and accordingly ushering them down predetermined paths. Potential is treated as a concept too abstract to be pursued, so is ignored in its entirety. Constant testing, grades, GPA, etc. reinforces this sentiment. As a result, those who display the brightest spark *at that moment in time* are those that reap the fruits offered by this system, the rest must settle. If we want to cater to a wider pool of students, we must change the system's core competency from identification to improvement. Let me make abundantly clear a fact every student knows, even those at the top, but seldom do educators accept—school is no longer a place to learn, it's a place to pass or fail.

Educational Apathy

This is probably the greatest crime of the educational system. Everything I've talked about culminates in the subliminal promotion of educational apathy. In other words, kids don't care about learning. It's seen as something they *have* to do, rather than *want* to do.

This is a miracle in its own right—we've somehow managed to suck out the willingness of children to do something they are biologically hardwired to do. Right from the moment we're born, the one thing we are designed to do is survive, making our ability to make sense of the world an innate drive. Still, by the end of twenty-two revolutions around the sun, the willingness to learn is sucked out of our very being.

How did this happen?

It began with the blatant disregard of three fundamental characteristics of human nature: curiosity, playfulness and sociability.[33]

Curiosity is why we're motivated to start doing something. It's why infants are fascinated by the most trivial things. It's why cultures worldwide are attracted to the unknown. It is why billions were spent exploring the globe, and now space.

Playfulness is how we improve. It's why a musician sits still to play the same song for hours on end. It's why video games are addictive. It's why the Olympics is one of the only successful feats of global cooperation we have achieved. Playfulness makes repeating the things we are curious about pleasurable, thereby allowing us to attain mastery of the basics and push the envelope, simultaneously.

Sociability is the reason the collective improves. When one learns, we all learn. It's why we have culture. It's why social media has reached the core of society. Our tendency to share information causes new knowledge to diffuse through groups, thereby increasing the knowledge level of all.

Now, curiosity and sociability are widely accepted, not utilized to great effect, but accepted nonetheless. However, ever since the conception of modern schooling, playfulness has been incrementally marginalized with every batch of students. Our decision-makers, regardless of their position on the political spectrum, collectively seem to agree that it's the quantity of time spent on academics in the classroom and at home that matter most to increase learning outcomes. For all the reasons mentioned thus far, this is incredibly naive, lazy, and simply incorrect.

So, why *play*? Let's start by looking at what it is.

As described by research professor Peter Gray, play is not binary. It's broad and tough to define. Better understood as a spectrum, an activity could be zero per cent play, hundred per cent play, or anything in between. It has everything to do with one's mentality during an act, and nothing to do with the act itself. One can be running around outside with other people and not be playing, while another can be sitting in a room typing away on a computer and be playing.

Moreover, play can be best identified through the existence of select characteristics when performing an activity. All don't have to be present to induce a playful experience but the more that emerge, the more playful the event. These can be boiled down to the following: intrinsically motivated, guided by implicit rules, self-chosen and self-directed, imaginative, and conducted with an alert but relaxed state of mind. I will now elaborate on each.[34]

First, play is *intrinsically motivated*. When we do something purely to realize the outcome, it's not play. For example, during any sporting tournament, even though the point is to win, if we simply hand the first-place trophy to one team, the satisfaction would be negligible compared to if the team went through the process of beating all the others. In this case, everyone is motivated by the joy of playing the game more than the joy of winning.

Likewise, when someone picks a job purely based on the pay, it quickly becomes an ever-increasing burden to perform the required tasks. They would most definitely not go to work if they were paid the same salary to sit at home. This is not play. When people say, 'Pick a career based on passion' or, 'If you do what you love, you'll never work a day in your life,' this is what they mean. Any activity performed by extrinsic motivation is not sustainable over a long time; it takes a massive toll on one's mind and body, thereby forcing one to achieve an outcome by doing the bare minimum. This might land you the cool first job, but it's a sure-fire method to ensure stagnation in one's career. For most, this also is why extracurricular activities don't count as play—participants never signed up for the intrinsic satisfaction it provides, but rather for the line item on their resume.

Second, Play is *guided by mental rules*. It's an activity that involves structure. The rules of the game must be clear in the player's mind, and he must act in adherence to them. If the rules are broken, the player who veered away is ousted, or the game ceases to exist—unless *all players* unanimously agree to change the rules. This is how play instills the art of self-control in children.

Third, play is *self-chosen and self-directed*. Even though one may not have complete freedom, it's an activity one opts to be part of and is allowed to quit at any time. The pleasure of play is derived from the liberty it inherently provides.

Often, amongst children, the very presence of an adult may hinder the emergence of play. As a parent, when you take your middle school kid to participate in a sporting event, it is not play—the child is a mere pawn in a pre-organized event; When we are coerced into or obligated to do something, it is not play. This seems obvious but is ignored by adults routinely. For example, in school, this is why gamification of subject material is rarely pleasurable to students; neither did they volunteer to participate nor are they allowed to quit.

Fourth, play is *imaginative*. In children, this is best exemplified by role-playing, where they alternate between fantasy and reality. In a fictional world is where children explore social boundaries without any fear, and where they develop the power to simulate reality in the mind. This is no trivial point. We frequently hear adults saying we must think creatively. However, creativity comes from imagination, which is developed through play. And yet, play is sacrificed.

A great example is the *Duncan's candle problem* experiment. Researchers gave participants a book of matches, a small candle and a box of tacks. Using only these items, they were tasked to attach the candle to a bulletin board so that it may be lit and burned properly. The problem was originally developed back in the 1940s, but in this study, prior to being given the problem, one group was made to watch a five-minute comedy film, another sat through a five-minute film on serious math, while the last watched nothing. The outcome was clear. The first group achieved a 75 per cent success rate while the other two achieved only a 20 per cent and 13 per cent success rate, respectively.[35]

Point is, the imaginative capacity of play is a powerful force when it comes to absorbing, assimilating, and analyzing information. Regardless of age, it allows us to access a state of mind that is incredibly adept for problem-solving, higher-level reasoning, emotional intelligence, and pretty much all complex endeavors.[36]

Lastly, play is *conducted with an alert but relaxed state of mind.* Considering the existence of rules, one must be actively present in whatever he is doing. However, the absence of external pressures doesn't allow the emergence of stress or any similar emotion. The mental state induced is eerily similar to what researchers now call *Flow*—a state of mind in which one loses all sense of time and is immersed in the activity at hand. They often consider it an ideal state for learning and creativity but never refer to it as play. I don't think we need a new term for it, but utilize these new learnings we must.

Okay, now that we have an idea of what play is, the simplicity of it all may be a source of skepticism for some in terms of its influence in education. Here, it's important to note that it's precisely that, which makes it so potent. Play definitely results in immense learning for the player but that's not why he plays. The joy of the activity is the motivator for the act, education is a by-product.

By no means does this mean it's easy—quite the contrary— because as soon as the challenge is lost, the activity becomes boring and loses its attractiveness (video games being the best example). However, the repetitiveness of doing the same activity with incremental difficulty leads to mastery. Every iteration of the act may systematically be the same, but each repetition allows the player to not only perfect the basics but also experiment novel solutions, thereby gaining a nuanced understanding of the skill.

Simply put, play *is* education. It may not seem like it on the surface but that's a feature, not a bug. In the failure of recognizing this relationship, children today are deprived of the fruits of play. Lack of it probably won't kill the physical body as would restriction to food, air, or water, but it does suppress mental growth.

Proof of its value can be seen by its omnipresence in all forms of life that is further ahead in brain growth, such as mammals and some species of birds. From an evolutionary perspective, to play freely is a biological drive that acts as nature's way of ensuring young mammals will practice and master skills essential to survive and thrive in the wild. In fact, its utility is so evident that one can deduce what type of play a species will carry out simply by observing the skill set they require to survive in adulthood. For example, predatory mammals play parallels stalking and hunting. Prey animals like gazelles play by sprinting and dodging; monkeys play by swinging around in trees. For us, play is our intrinsic ability to improve at the art of being human. Amongst our species, social play is by design a continuous exercise in cooperation, mutually beneficial decision making, and consideration of the needs of others—all which are arguably cornerstones of civilisation.[37]

Given the importance of play, the numbers are quite abysmal.

∽

- From 1981 to 1997, children aged 6-8 spent 18 per cent more time in school, 145 per cent more time on homework, 55 per cent less time conversing with others at home and 25 per cent less time *playing*.[38]
  - In a follow-up study, conducted from 1997 to 2003, time spent on homework increased by 32 per cent, and play further *decreased* by 7 per cent.[39]

- Amongst high school students, 66 per cent said that they were bored in class every day.[40]
  - When asked why, 82 per cent of students said that the material wasn't interesting, and 41 per cent said that the material wasn't relevant.
- Amongst middle school students: 36 per cent of the time they were bored was while doing schoolwork.[41]
- According to a Gates Foundation study, boredom ranked first among reasons why high school students decide to drop out.[42]
- Amongst college students, 59 per cent were bored during half or more of their lectures, and only 2 per cent said that none of their lectures were boring.[43]
  - This explains why 25-40 per cent of students don't even go to class.[44]

Steven Pinker, a Harvard professor and renowned author, had this to say:

> A few weeks into every semester, I face a lecture hall that is half-empty, despite the fact that I am repeatedly voted a Harvard Yearbook Favorite Professor, that the lectures are not video-recorded, and that they are the only source of certain material that will be on the exam. I don't take it personally; it's common knowledge that Harvard students stay away from lectures in droves, burning a fifty-dollar bill from their parents' wallets every time they do.[45]

∽

Knowing all this, it's no surprise that school is where children are least happy. And here is where the foundation is laid for all future behavior.

In K-12 education, by restricting play we foster an attitude that children learn primarily by doing adult-directed and adult-evaluated tasks, and their own activities are worthless. So, when children go to

A prepared student?

college—a place where many possess ungodly amounts of free time—they come to the conclusion that the grade is all that is needed. The implicit message is, 'If you do what you're told, everything will work out for you.' Those who buy into this, stop taking responsibility for their own education under the false assumption that the path to becoming a successful adult has been figured out. Inevitably, when the cards are non-deterministically dealt, those that did everything right become the victim—'My life is messed up because school/parents/society failed me.' And those who never were the 'good' students, find themselves trapped in a cycle of mediocrity. In other words, if the institution of learning itself is telling individuals that learning isn't their cup of tea, and their reality affirms that sentiment, why in the bloody world would they pursue it further?

Overall, schooling is extrinsically motivated through grades, carried out in a state of mind that is far from relaxed and, most definitely, is not done voluntarily. If anything, school conveys to students that learning is fundamentally opposite to play. This is dangerous. We take away the pleasure of the activity; this naturally leads to apathy.

At the end of the day, learning is only possible when one desires to learn. And the reality is that childhood is no longer seen as a time for learning as much as a time for resume building. It's no secret. Kids know this. More importantly, that's all they've ever known. Their whole lives, learning—or, school-related work—has always been mutually exclusive to pleasure, justified by the sentiment: 'Otherwise you won't go to a good college or get a good job'. So, how can we blame them when they don't see the point of learning? Especially if resumes can and are built by superficial means—rote memory, extracurricular activity stacking and so forth. This might work for a handful at getting into college or a job, but as we can already see by our polarized global order, it can have severe negative long-term effects on the individual and society.

What is really amazing is that all this is happening in spite of learning being one of the few natural highs provided to us alongside the gift of life. And still, in the name of education, we refuse to use this to our advantage. It's crazy! One can *literally* get addicted to learning. I got addicted after two decades on this planet. Others have too, I've seen it! Now, I'm not an advocate for addictions of any kind but I must confess, this is an addiction we must not only encourage children towards but also guide them through the process of attaining. I believe I speak for all when I say a learning addiction is something we can be proud of, and more importantly, is going to be vital for civil life moving forward into the 21st century.

Part 3

The Future

'The amount of time we spend thinking we can't,
is more than enough time to learn how we can'
-Yours Truly

17

Now what?

Education is probably the most influential factor in determining how one's life is going to pan out. So, it pays to know everything there is to know about it. Chances are it will come in handy at least once in your life—may it be for your kid, a family member, or a friend. Considering I've just bombarded you with all that is wrong with our education system, it would only be right to end with practical information to deal with this problem going forward.

Unfortunately, the people making real progress simply don't get the necessary attention for them to make the impact we all wish for them to have. In fact, there very well may be those that don't get any attention at all. Therefore, I will briefly introduce you to people and initiatives that, at the least, I am aware of, so you may get a glimpse of what holds real potential moving into the future.

Important to note that none of the following options are panaceas. They are nothing but initiatives people are currently working on to address the many issues in education.

Sudbury Schools

These are the K-12 schools that follow a pedagogical philosophy first used at Sudbury Valley School in Massachusetts, USA. Established in 1968, it's a model that believes that learning is self-initiated, self-motivated and a by-product of all human activity.

Their curriculum demands students to take responsibility for their own education by giving them full jurisdiction over what to do with their time. There is no predetermined syllabus. Children learn by exploring their interests, academic or otherwise, by the free exchange of ideas between students of all ages, and the guidance provided by faculty. Yes, there is no age-based division and this results in a mutually beneficial dynamic; the youngins learn from the older students and vice versa.

I acknowledge this may seem incredibly radical and contrarian to what you've seen in mainstream K-12 education. But regardless of whether it's objectively better or worse—and in all honesty, they have their critics—the fact that such initiatives are being accepted and utilized in several schools worldwide says a lot about the status quo and the need for innovation.

Montessori Education

Brought to life by Maria Montessori in 1907, this pedagogy is best described by her:

> I studied the children, and they taught me how to teach them.[1]

This is another child-centered form of education that closely parallels the philosophies of the Sudbury Schools and has been used worldwide for over a century. Granted, this pedagogy is designed more for primary and middle school.

Finland

The education system in Finland is yet another example of how stringent restrictions are not an inevitable prerequisite to foster learning. This system is widely accepted as one of the world's most effective and successful systems when it comes to student outcomes. And, guess what? Hardly any standardized tests, shorter school hours and minimal emphasis on homework.

There are definitely other characteristics—such as students retaining the same teacher over the course of many years—that make their pedagogy so potent. But even the aforementioned differences alone are powerful signals that everyone can learn from when attempting to improve education.

Sugata Mitra

The next underrepresented force of nature I would like to introduce you to is Sugata Mitra. After specializing in the hard sciences, the potential efficacy of technology to improve education quickly took over his life.

He became known for his experiment, *Hole in the Wall*, where he embedded computers in the walls of rural areas in India, and allowed children to freely use it. Much to his surprise, children who had never interacted with computers before, in a matter of days, were not only utilizing several applications productively but also teaching what they had learned to their peers.

He later replicated this experiment internationally and demonstrated that groups of children—regardless of fluency in English and cultural or geographical backgrounds—can learn to harness the computer and the internet without any guidance, given the appropriate environment. Using these learnings, he refined his findings into a methodology now known as *Minimally Invasive Education*, which has the potential to significantly drive down costs in providing wholesome basic education to anyone, anywhere in the world.

Big Picture Learning

This is yet another curriculum that is learner-focused. In other words, they put students at the center of their own learning. The following is straight from their website:

Each student at a Big Picture Learning school is part of a small learning community of 15 students called an advisory. Each advisory is supported and led by an advisor, a teacher that works closely with the group of students and forms personalized relationships with each advisee... Each student works closely with his or her advisor to identify interests and personalize learning. The student as the center of learning truly engages and challenges the student and makes learning authentic and relevant.[2]

Their model has been so successful that it has been adopted by schools worldwide.[3]

Khan Academy

Of course, no discussion about the future of education can ever be complete without mentioning Khan Academy. For those who've been living under a rock, Khan Academy is a 100 per cent free, online resource, started by Salman Khan of Louisiana in 2008. It began as a giant aggregation of video lectures on YouTube, covering a wide range of topics taught in traditional K-12 schools. After this caught traction, he created a relatively simple piece of software—simple in hindsight, that is—that solves one of the key issues plaguing education today, the absence of Mastery Learning. The lecturer never could disseminate information at a pace optimal for every student. The software attempts to solve this discrepancy.

It did this by providing teachers with real-time insight into the concepts each student is struggling with, thereby allowing teachers to maximize the productivity of every second within the classroom. Students who felt stuck could be focused on, while students who had sped ahead could learn more on their own via video lectures, or practice what they learned by becoming temporary teachers themselves.

At first glance, this may not sound very revolutionary, but it is. Here's why: from the beginning of structured education, the predominant method of teaching was lecture-based. The key point to remember is that the lecture model is extremely convenient for the teacher, but never was a robust model for the learner. Khan Academy's resources allow the teacher to conduct the class with the same convenience, *but put the learner's needs first.* The large bank of quality video lectures eradicated the need for the in-class lecture as students can now access quality lectures on new concepts anytime and anywhere; and active learning by solving problems can be done with the newly-freed-up class time. This, coupled with real-time insight into where each student is struggling, empowers teachers to degrees never before possible.

If schools are considering adopting this technology, they should do so without wasting any more time. It is a no-brainer. There is nothing to lose, but everything to gain. The guy is literally giving it for free! If this software lives up to its potential, people will look back at this point in time and regard it as one of the most crucial moments in the history of human civilization. What a time to be alive.

Minerva Schools at KGI

Minerva is probably one of the best things to happen in the higher education landscape today. A new university with the mission to become the best.

Even though it is still a four-year program, there are key differences that accomplish the goal of student learning with much greater efficacy than what is done by the incumbents. For example, through the course of one's undergraduate journey, students live in a different city—ranging from San Francisco to Seoul—every semester. Another is their effective use of technology to impart knowledge. They don't resort to hiring more faculty to expand their tuition revenue stream, they connect existing professors via their proprietary platform called the *Active Learning Forum*. And not to mention, all at a price-point less than traditional undergraduate programs as they have no overhead in the form of gyms, fields, large administration departments, and other facilities which contribute nothing to student learning.

This is all just the tip of the iceberg. The truly amazing element of this institute, I believe, is their push to challenge the status quo. A much-needed step that I hope is only the first.

18

What should I do?

Is K-12 worth it?

The verdict on K-12 is pretty clear. In spite of all its flaws, don't drop out! Get through it by any means necessary. The stigma that comes with being a high school dropout is like shooting yourself in the foot before the longest marathon of your life—your life.

For parents, I suggest encouraging kids to do their best in school, remembering to take a step back the second it starts to become a physical burden on them. Unlike in earlier eras, the value of grades has significantly depreciated. Attaining high scores is simply not worth the immense toll it can take on childhood. A much better use of time is to allow your child to find something they truly enjoy, because only when they discover their own interests will excellence be in the realm of possibility.

As a corollary to this, I understand how some may be skeptical due to the observation that whenever children get free time, they tend to resort to video games and other such unproductive activities. This is only so because of the subliminal coercion their mind is jostling with every day. In other words, when they are forced to go to school and engage in activities they have no intrinsic motivation towards, the primal response is to be free from the figurative shackles. And the activities you view as unproductive are nothing but a source of liberation for the child. This is why they can't wait to go home to play videogames, watch YouTube videos or whatever else it may be.

In the non-traditional education world, this is normal. It's a phase known as *deschooling:*[1] the adjustment period kids face when they first get pulled out of traditional school. Think of it as acclimatization to the real world, during which one rediscovers agency and curiosity.

Often, when children suddenly find themselves with nothing but free time (due to the absence of any obligations) they resort to spending it on whatever activities they were doing before. However, depending on how long a child spent in traditional schooling, they soon realize that they are only doing so because they themselves chose to do it. Not due to any external (albeit subliminal) stimulus. This epiphany proceeds with the realization that there is an infinite array of activities that they can pursue *simply because they want to.* This is how innate curiosity, once again, bubbles up to the surface and acts as a compass to guide the child through the journey that is lifelong learning. It truly is a beautiful sight to see.

Note: This is not an attempt to convince anyone to abandon traditional schooling—only a reminder of its weaknesses. Adaptation is required if setting your child up for success is a goal you value.

Is Higher Education worth it?

When it comes to higher education, the two main elements you need to consider are affordability and expectation. Below is a table of most of the likely combinations. My goal is to provide you with a framework to approach the question, not give you *your* unique answer. That would be impossible. Every situation is different. Nonetheless, I hope it helps.

SHOULD I GO TO COLLEGE?
TAKING A LOAN?
NO
YES
WHATS THE EXPECTATION FROM COLLEGE?
TO FIGURE OUT LIFE
WHATS THE EXPECTATION FROM COLLEGE?
I WANT TO BE AN ENTERPRENEUR
I JUST REALLY NEED A LICENSE?
GO
I WANT TO BE AN ENTERPRENEUR
I JUST REALLY NEED A LICENSE?
UP TO YOU
I KNOW WHAT I WANT AND IT'S IN HIGH DEMAND
UP TO YOU
TO FIGURE OUT LIFE
OK GO
I KNOW WHAT I WANT TO DO!
I KNOW WHAT I WANT AND IT'S IN LOW DEMAND
DOES IT NEED A LICENSE?
IS IT HIGH IN DEMAND?
DON'T GO
DOES IT NEED A LICENSE?
NO
YES
NO
YES
NO
YES
UP TO YOU
UP TO YOU
DOES IT NEED A LICENSE?
UP TO YOU
GO
NO
YES
DOES IT NEED A LICENSE?
DON'T GO
UP TO YOU
NO
YES
GO

I Need Loans

Expectation	Verdict	Remember
I want to figure out what to do in life	Don't go!	B, D, E, F
I know what I want to do, it's in high demand and doesn't need licensing.	Up to you.	A, B, C, E
I know what I want to do, it's in low demand and doesn't need licensing.	Don't go!	B, D, E, F
I need licensing.	Go.	A, B, C, E
I want to be an entrepreneur.	Don't go!	B, D, E, G

I Don't Need Loans

Expectation	Verdict	Remember
I want to figure out what to do in life.	Go.	B, C, E
I know what I want to do, it's in high demand and doesn't need licensing.	Up to you.	B, C, E
I know what I want to do, it's in low demand and doesn't need licensing.	Up to you.	B, C, E
I need licensing.	Go.	B, C, E
I want to be an entrepreneur.	Up to you.	B, C, E, G

Remember

A. Minimize Costs

Unlike what student debt statistics might imply, attaining a college education doesn't have to be as big a financial burden as it may seem. Expenses rack up, but only because individuals often make poor decisions. Picking a college based on how attractive the campus is, the geographical location, where your friends go or other such superficial factors, are some examples of how many end up making decisions at the expense of their future. This is stupid. Don't do it. Instead, make minimizing costs your top priority. For most, obtaining the degree is what pays, not how you obtain it.

Here are a few options you can consider:

1. Go to community college for the first two-years and then transfer to a degree-granting institute.
2. Invest time in identifying and applying to all possible scholarships.
3. Some European countries offer free or almost-free higher education to international citizens as well. Research and consider all your options.[2]

B. Use Time Productively

If you do end up going to college, know that you're never going to get another four years with so much free time again. Use it wisely. These are the years that will dictate the trajectory your life will take. An extremely common mistake is to have blind faith in the degree. Don't fall victim to this fallacy. Most trod along their college journey with the assumption that everything will work out with the degree by their side, and after graduating, they struggle to make any movement with regard to their aspirations because they get caught in the trenches of the battle against short-term necessities: shelter, food, actually being employable, etc.

There are many ways one can use their time productively, especially in today's day and age. Many high-value skills (content creation, writing, coding, SEO, digital marketing, web design, etc.) only require a computer/smartphone and the internet to develop. My suggestion is to try as many as you can, as quickly as you can, and see what clicks (*spoiler*: most won't). After which, double down on what seems to be working and get really good at it.

Bottom line: Actively develop new skills.

This brings me to another great way to spend massive amounts of free time. Directed primarily at the ambitious ones, maybe start a business? Today, the barrier to enter the online business space is at an all-time low. Leverage it! Even if it may not be something you want to pursue in the long term, the experience will help you for the rest of your life. Think about it like this: if you ever get a job, chances are the entity that hires you is going to be an existing business. So, if you're educated on the principles of how businesses function, you will have a disproportionate advantage over your competition. You will be able to understand the business, and provide maximal value (which could also increase your salary).

C. Leverage College Resources

This is self-explanatory. Colleges have existing relationships with alumni and employers. Not to mention, a plethora of resources to achieve clarity on almost every doubt or problem you may have. Use them.

D. Unfavorable Risk

The seemingly blind trust our society has in traditional higher education is a symptom of another fallacy propagated to the youth by authority figures. Throughout childhood, we're reminded that when we grow up, we can do anything, have anything and be anything our heart desires. Now, while I agree with the sentiment, it often leads students to make very unwise decisions. The truth is, you can't have *everything*. Not because of inadequacies with the individual, but because of the laws of physics. As the saying goes: 'if you don't sacrifice for what you want, what you want becomes the sacrifice'.

Given that this is true (I still haven't found a human who can be in two places simultaneously), you literally cannot have both. Instead, to keep morale up, I believe a better message for kids is this,

> 'You can most certainly have many of the things you care about,
> just not all at the same time.'

So, with expectations raised artificially high, when it comes to the decision of college, promises are made liberally—learn whatever you want, have the time of your life, grow up, secure a job—to name a few. But due to the absence of key caveats in the student's mind, college is viewed as a golden ticket into the life that was 'promised'. As we've seen, this isn't the case, which makes financing college by student loans a very risky bet. Remember, there is a reason why gambling is a multi-billion-dollar industry. Chances are, you will lose.

If college doesn't pan out as expected, you will be stuck under a mountain of debt that can easily eat up a decade of your life, at the least. You won't be able to make any progress towards your dreams and aspirations—personal, financial, spiritual or whatever it may be. Understand indentured servitude and know it can become a real possibility. If history is any predictor of the future, I highly recommend you watch the countless videos uploaded on the internet by the victims of student debt themselves.

Lastly (this point may seem obvious, but I've heard it way too many times), often due to easy access to loans, many consider it to be free money. It is not. I repeat, a student loan is NOT free money. You will pay for it with your future.

E. Focus On Self-Discovery

Due to the abstract nature of the concept, I must start by saying that everyone's path will be different—there is no right or wrong way. That said, for it to be achieved, you must actively pay attention. The funny thing about learning about yourself is that we expect it to happen in school. And it's funny because, in spite of more than a decade of school, I made zero progress towards this goal. However, after two-years of explicitly focusing on my interests, I found more clarity than I ever had. This made me think. Why are many students coming out of college with no sense of direction (mind you, I'm not talking about a complete life plan).

I believe this is because of our reliance on being the object, not subject. Put another way, we've overbought into destiny. The fallacy perpetuated by the romance of destiny is one that I, too, was a victim of and wish upon no one. The media and, importantly, the mere convenience makes it all too easy for one, especially children, to adopt the fantasy of destiny as a core value. Then they base their life around it—don't fall for this trap. It disincentivizes initiative, without which, don't expect anything in your reality to change for the better. The fact that schools don't push this mode of thinking, as opposed to whatever is demanded by college, is a great crime.

On another note, one of the biggest traps I fell for is confusing fascination for passion. A good way to address this issue is by taking inspiration from the scientific method. In other words, form a hypothesis—whatever you think you would enjoy doing for the rest of your life—dedicate a good amount of time, and if you find yourself struggling to be consistent, restart the process with something else. Here, consistency is key. You will accomplish nothing within a short period of time. Don't mistake things that give you dopamine (the *feel-good* chemical your brain produces as a reward mechanism) for things you love!

Finally, since humans are complex systems, our interests are dynamic—there is always a possibility for them to change, thus making self-discovery a lifelong process. Point is, even if you are certain, it's always a good practice to avoid making absolute statements regarding your future. This helps us avoid the sunk-cost fallacy. In other words, the fact that you've invested large amounts of time and energy into something isn't a reason for you to stick to it. If changing your focus is the right decision now, the resources already spent are irrelevant. Don't let it make you change-averse.

F. Save First

If you're extremely passionate about a field and dream of studying it in college, then great! You just found yourself a long-term goal. Most people struggle to identify what they want to work towards, so they resort to material possessions. And then, frequently wonder why nothing is ever enough.

Use this goal as fuel to motivate you through the inevitable hard work, save up, and then fulfil all that your heart desires.

G. Nothing Beats The Real World

Entrepreneurship is one of the most nuanced journeys one can choose to pursue. This makes it inconceivably difficult to learn in an artificial environment. College can only offer an abstraction of the real thing, which in most cases, is inferior. You will undoubtedly learn more about how to be successful by doing than sitting in a classroom.

Of course, this doesn't mean you shouldn't learn everything there is to learn about business. In fact, you must, if you wish to have any shot at success. But the beauty of being alive today is that you have the internet and books. There is almost nothing you cannot learn from these two resources. Use them. That said, a large part of being a successful entrepreneur is the team. Here, college has the potential to be incredibly powerful.

∽

There is one caveat to all this. If the college you've been accepted into is a top college (i.e. Ivy leagues, Stanford, etc.), then it's almost always the correct decision to go because (1) of the brand name associated, and (2) the concentration of talent will open doors that are simply impossible to find elsewhere.

Some might claim hypocrisy by my suggestion to conform in spite of being so critical of the system. This is only so because traditional education is a great accelerator. Kicker is, it's blind—it'll accelerate one in the right or wrong path. And today, the variables are such that many can't afford the costs associated with having taken the wrong path. So, beware.

In conclusion, considering I too was an eighteen-year-old not long ago, I am well aware that many will still do what they want—in spite of everything I've mentioned in this book. Don't be that kid! But still, you might (I was), and for you, I have one more piece of advice. Do what your heart desires, but keep in mind everything you have learned here. It took me three years in college to recognize its inadequacies, and by then, it was too late for me to rip the bandage off. But I hope that when you realize the truth in what I am saying, don't hesitate to cut your losses. It is simply not worth it to sacrifice the next decade of your life to fulfill a four-year fantasy that society has embedded in your mind.

How do I leverage self-education?

In culmination to the, hopefully, valuable journey you've been through while reading this book, I want to provide you with a framework that will enable you to take learning into your own hands. As we've seen, education is too important a factor to be reliant on institutes with dubious incentive structures. And the most beautiful thing about being alive today is that this independence not only is possible, but also can be much more cost-effective—provided you know what to do.

I went through the iterative process of making mistakes, hitting walls, working my way to understanding and found myself using this general process, over the past four years.

It won't give you complete clarity regarding how you should do everything, but it will most definitely enlighten you on what you should be doing. In other words, it won't give you answers on a platter, it'll give you direction as to how to attain those answers. Of course, I myself still have a lot to learn, but this advice will undoubtedly save you years—should you choose to implement it.

That said, I present to you...

A PRACTICAL GUIDE TO MASTERING SELF-EDUCATION (without spending $1000s)

Step 1: Be Educable

Learning begins with possessing the ability to be educated. In other words, since learning is a physical activity, you need a whole lot of high-quality energy. Just like going to the gym with a body that has been sedentary will not be a very pleasant experience, trying to learn without having your physical and mental-wellbeing in order will be a handicap, right from the get-go. Some may be cynical and blame their innate inability to learn after multiple failed attempts—assuming that if they could, they would be able to do so with relative ease, just like the class genius. This is a fallacy.

It is unwise to compare yourself with someone who has started with tools under their belt that you simply don't have. For us common folk, getting our body fit is a necessity to learn. This is probably one of the most important factors that everybody overlooks. They jump straight into trying to absorb new information and then wonder why they don't seem to make any progress. It's because you're trying to climb a mountain with a large f**king boulder on your shoulders.

How do we get rid of this boulder? You must kick-start a feedback loop that begins in the mind. It's impossible to get your body in order without having a strong mind; however, once you make progress on your physical fitness, it will automatically strengthen the mind. Let me illustrate by example. Have you, for no objective reason, suddenly been flooded by emotions that can be best described as *those that make you avoid doing what you should be doing*? Minimal control over one's emotions is a sign of a weak mind. This usually leads to desiring a dopamine hit; we do something that feels good in the moment. Suffice to say, this is counterproductive when trying to accomplish a long-term task, like becoming physically fit. You cannot afford to have your mental state easily swayed by randomness. Thick skin towards the plethora of stimuli is what you need to cultivate. This can be done by controlling three simple variables: your diet, sleep, and environment.

Diet is a powerful factor because it is your primary source of energy. It determines the quantity and quality of energy your brain has to work with. If you're still skeptical, I suggest you read up on the *Gut-Brain Connection*.

Sleep is equally powerful. When you sleep, your body recovers. It eliminates the large quantities of mental fog that often makes bad decisions seem good in the moment. I suggest picking up *Why We Sleep* by Matthew Walker, for more on this topic.

The environment, too, can influence your mental condition in inconceivable ways. A good example is peer pressure—the phenomenon of investing time and energy into actions solely based on the people around you. Similarly, if you have a very chaotic environment (messy room, negative people, etc.), you will find it much harder to focus.

Once you make headway towards achieving mental clarity, you can begin with physical exercise. Here, I don't mean high-intensity workouts. At the bare minimum, you only need to get your heart rate up for about thirty to forty minutes every day. I go for a quick run. Over time, when you do this consistently, you will observe your mental condition improving as well, thus kick-starting a positive feedback loop.

Now you are educable. You may move onto Step 2.

Step 2: Remember The Principles

By no means is this an exhaustive list. It's only an aggregation of those I've come across that pertain to effective learning. Based on my experience, many will help in other facets of your life as well.

Check for expiration dates!

It's funny, we always check for expiration dates when we go to the grocery store. Then, why do we forget to do the same when it comes to the equally important act of education?

As it stands today, our schools have long since expired. As a natural consequence, the information people use in their day-to-day life has expired too. To combat this, I haven't found a fool proof method, only heuristics. For one, stress-test everything and actively look for criticism. If you come across new information, don't assume it's correct until you have identified and analyzed all the assumptions. Often, when an assumption is no longer valid, the conclusion follows in its footsteps. Another method you could use is to simply ask the experts *who love their field*. They tend to make it a point to be aware of all the latest developments.

Prioritize what has endured

In a world where change is perpetual in some form or the other, it's a much better use of time to identify and learn what has endured. As Mr Taleb says:

> We know a lot more what is wrong than what is right... negative knowledge (what is wrong, what does not work) is more robust to error than positive knowledge (what is right, what works). So knowledge grows by subtraction much more than by addition— given that what we know today might turn out to be wrong, but what we know to be wrong cannot turn out to be right, at least not easily.[3]

In other words, there is a category of knowledge that grows when we learn what is false. This is the category you want to prioritize; it has the largest likelihood of not becoming obsolete throughout the course of your life. This is the same principle that makes the maxim, 'Keeping one's distance from the ignorant is equivalent to keeping company with the wise,' as true as ever.

A good way of identifying knowledge of this nature is by asking two questions. (1) How long has it survived? and, (2) How many solutions are there to the problem it solves? You want the answer to first question to be maximal i.e., very long, and the second, as few as possible. Of course, this is no foolproof method; you must adapt it to your situation.

Make new mistakes, fast

Mistakes are inevitable when learning something new. In fact, making mistakes is often a sign that you're actually making progress, as long as you don't repeat the same ones over and over again. Therefore, the faster you make them, the faster you will learn. Come to terms with this. Every time you get stuck or hit a wall of some sort, remember that it's a good thing. It means you are one step closer to proficiency. This will make those failures slightly more bearable.

Ideally, you should learn vicariously. This is not impossible, but I recognize it is difficult to execute, especially for younger people. Experiential learning, for some reason, always tends to last longer. After all, that is how we've learned for many millennia.

Learning deceives

This is not objectively true, but the general idea holds water. Which is, you need to see it through to the end if the benefits are what you wish to reap. To internalize this principle, you must first understand the nature of exponential growth. Most, including myself, are easily deceived because it's very counterintuitive to how our brains have evolved. For perspective, let me ask you the famous lily pad question: In a pond, there is a lily pad that reproduces into two every day. Each new lily pad does the same. By day thirty, the entire pond will be covered in lily pads. My question to you is, on which day will it be half-full?

Most people intuitively think it's around day fifteen. However, the correct answer is day 29. Even though I told you that the lily pads double every day, it's still extremely counterintuitive to wrap your brain around the fact that the pond is half-full *the day before* it is full. This is what makes exponential growth so tricky—and powerful.

If we apply the same concept to learning, if you stop at day twenty-nine, you've essentially cut your learning in half. If you stop at day twenty-eight, you've missed out on 75 per cent. Moral of the story: get to the end by any means necessary. Furthermore, think of learning not as a single, but a series of exponential curves. Because, theoretically, learning never ends. So, when we hit the figurative day twenty-eight or twenty-nine of learning—the point colloquially referred to as the knee of the curve—we say it *clicked*. Which then puts us on a new curve for the subsequent topic.

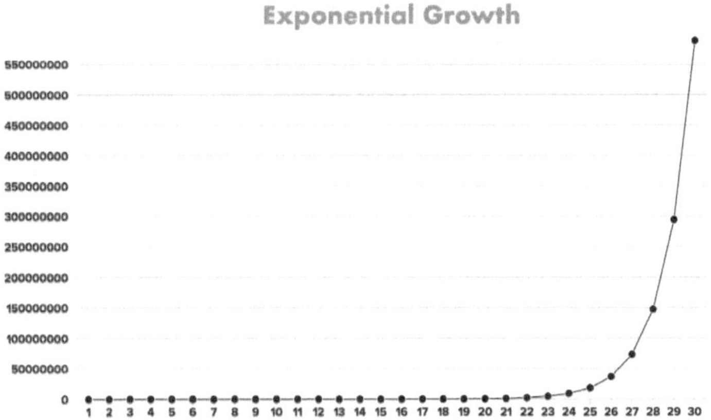

Additionally, it's the exponential nature of learning that makes it so easy to quit at the early stages. Almost always, the decision is binary, we choose to learn or not. However, we make an incorrect assumption when we weigh the two options. We think, (1) we can spend the time on learning, which due to the deceivingly slow growth at the early stages, will reciprocate with very little value. Or (2) we can spend the time on another activity, which might reciprocate with immediate pleasure.

Naturally, we compare the two outcomes and pick the latter. But due to our inadequate understanding of opportunity cost, this comparison is incomplete. You see, the time spent on learning not only reciprocates with the little value received today but also moves you one step closer to the knee of the curve. This is pretty difficult to accurately value, so we ignore it altogether. Suffice to say, this rationale repeats itself every time we try to learn something new.

Another common obstacle that arises due to the exponential nature of learning is our inability to see immediate effects. This is abundantly evident when trying to enlighten people on the value of reading books. The book is never going to bear fruit the day after reading it, it's only going to do so after months, maybe years, as life goes on. We incorrectly assume that since we aren't seeing the benefits that were promised, in spite of the act of learning fresh in our mind, what we're doing must be wrong or useless. So we quit. This is a trap. To avoid it, never forget that the effects of what you learn will only manifest after the memory of the act of learning has been forgotten.[4]

Leverage iterative processes

The iterative process is a fundamental methodology through which entities grow.

Action → Effect → Action based on preceding effect → Effect →
Action based...

Think of it as nature's way of using data in decision making, best exemplified by evolution. However, just like it, many of the strongest forces for change are iterative processes. In learning, we call the iterative process 'practice'.

Personally, I always wondered why everybody told me to practice. I could see that it worked, but never committed 100 per cent to it because neither did I want to invest the massive amount of effort it required, nor did I understand what made it unique. Being lazy, I actively sought out other low-effort solutions to learning. This was fine for school since I didn't really care about it, but now, after understanding the rationale, practice has been a strategy that has never failed me.

Set accountability mechanisms

Relying on your willpower is not impossible, but it will fail you sooner or later. Therefore, it's always a good idea to have an accountability system that acts as an external motivator to ensure you do what you need to do. This could be anything from setting a common goal with a friend, to hiring someone for this explicit reason. Humans are incentive-driven machines. Create incentives for yourselves.

Take action in spite of feeling unprepared

When learning something new, you will seldom feel prepared to get into the crux of the material. But you must. We tend to avoid it because it seems daunting at first glance, but without making an attempt, no amount of information-absorption will make us learn better. Simply put, you can only feel prepared when you have learned, but to learn you need to do; doing is a prerequisite to preparation, not vice versa.

Kill limiting beliefs

Carol Dweck, a professor of psychology at Stanford, conducted a simple experiment in the mid-1990s with the hypothesis that differing forms of praise would have an insignificant effect on learning outcomes. It was as follows: Almost 400 fifth-graders were given a basic nonverbal test. After the tests were graded and returned, the researchers provided each student with a single line of feedback; a random half were praised for their intelligence (e.g. 'You must be smart at this'), while the others were praised for effort (e.g. 'You must have worked really hard'). Then, the students were made to choose between an easy and difficult test. Surprisingly, around 90 per cent of the kids who were praised for effort picked the difficult test, while the majority of kids who were praised for intelligence picked the easier one.

Next, she gave them all a test appropriate for eighth-graders. The students who were praised for intelligence gave up easily. The others pushed through. After this, the students were given a choice to look at the exam answers of those who did better, or who did worse. Interestingly, the students praised for intelligence almost always picked the latter, while those praised for effort picked the former. Lastly, the students were given a test of similar difficulty as the initial test. Intuitively, one would assume that the results would not be very different this time around. Surprisingly, those praised for effort did 30 per cent better, while those praised for intelligence did 20 per cent worse.[5]

What does this imply?

It shows us that when kids think it's the outcome from which their value is derived, it disincentives' risk-taking and mistakes, which inevitably sacrifices learning. This is what Dweck calls a *fixed mindset*—a mentality where one believes intellect is static and improvement is impossible. On the flip side, she refers to acting based on effort as the source of value as having a *growth mindset*—a mentality which makes the belief that improvement is possible, a catalyst to improvement.

I bring this up because it unequivocally shows not only the power of the mindset with which you approach learning, but also the influence of limiting beliefs—ideas that we believe to be true, often based on false conclusions, that constrain us is some way. One such belief is the assumption that things will stay the way they are—may it be learning ability or general circumstance. As a student of history, I can tell you that this is simply not true. Change is one of the few universal constants that have endured since the beginning of time, and will undoubtedly continue to do so.

A natural next question is, 'When it comes to learning, how can we catalyze this change?' Well, information is key. As we've seen, intelligence is neither static nor innate, but a highly dynamic

Yuval Noah Harari

'Humans certainly have a will-but it isn't free. You cannot decide what desires you have. You don't decide to be introvert or extrovert, easy-going or anxious, gay or straight. Humans make choices-but they are never independent choices.'

characteristic. Some may be born with an aptitude to catch on relatively quickly, but certainly don't possess pre-built knowledge. *Intellect is never an intrinsic characteristic.* Even the Einstein's and Musk's of the world, at one point, only knew what you know. A vital difference, however, is the information they consumed thereafter. This certainly made no sense to me the first time I heard it, so let me go further on this point.

You—your life, as it stands today, is nothing but the sum total of your decisions. And your decisions are a product of your thoughts. So far, so good. Here's where it gets tricky. Most people believe their thoughts are a product of their own free will. This is false. Thoughts think themselves (I won't spend time convincing you why this is so; it is well out of the scope of this book and its author. I was enlightened to this fact by Yuval Harari and Sam Harris,[6] so those are good places to start if you wish to learn more). As a sneak peek, here's an excerpt from Harari's article in *The Guardian:*

> Humans certainly have a will—but it isn't free. You cannot decide what desires you have. You don't decide to be introvert or extrovert, easy-going or anxious, gay or straight. Humans make choices—but they are never independent choices. Every choice depends on a lot of biological, social, and personal conditions that you cannot determine for yourself. I can choose what to eat, whom to marry and whom to vote for, but these choices are determined in part by my genes, my biochemistry, my gender, my family background, my national culture, etc.—and I didn't choose which genes or family to have.[7]

So then, what determines our thoughts? One answer is the sum total of the information we have consumed; whether through sight, sound, touch, smell or taste.

Grossly simplified, there is no free will, only a subconscious. And our subconscious has been molded since the day we were born by what we've been exposed to. Critically, it isn't absolute; over time, you can shape it however you like. But to do so, you must be thoughtful about where and how you spend your time. Ever heard the saying, 'Show me your friends and I'll show you your future?' What about, 'You're the average of the five people you spend the most time with?' This is what makes these sentiments true. If you still don't believe me, I hope you listen to Warren Buffet and Bill Gates.

> You will move in the direction of the people that you associate with. So it's important to associate with people who are better than yourself.[8]

This certainly doesn't mean blindly stop being friends with your friends—it might, if you realize they are the ones dragging you down. But more often than not, such drastic measures are not what you want to implement right off the bat. Instead, start by simply being mindful of the people you interact with, the food you eat, the news you watch, the social media you consume, the books you read, the music you listen to—you get the point. In the short-run, you probably won't see much difference. But the fact remains, it is one of the most robust mechanisms we have to catalyze change. Use it.

So, coming back to learning, every genius, billionaire and Olympian to-date, has only become successful because of all the information they've consumed. Which, naturally, is only but the work put in by those who came before them. So, don't let your current state or an incorrect idea of intellect discourage you. Everything in this book can be traced back to other great thinkers. None of today's tech-giants would exist without the internet; the internet wouldn't exist without the computer; the computer wouldn't exist without electricity; Einstein wouldn't be Einstein if not for Newton. And Newton himself said, 'If I have seen further, it is by standing on the shoulders of Giants.'[9] Truth is, *we all stand on the shoulders of giants.*

Morals of the story: (1) Be ruthless while filtering the information that hits your five senses, and (2) as Mr Ford knew a long time ago,

'Whether you think you can, or you think you can't—you're right.'

Hard work is inevitable

I define hard work as tasks that you don't want to do, but must be done regardless. We've all heard the saying, 'If you do what you love, it won't feel like work'. While I agree with the sentiment, at a micro-scale, it isn't as true. In other words, yes, you must identify goals as per your heart's guidance. However, in order to get there, you will quickly realize that there are tasks that must be accomplished, tasks without which your long-term goal will remain unattainable. This is what I refer to as hard work. It is inevitable. The same applies to learning. For example, if you want to get good at a sport, you first need to get your fitness in order; if you want to learn to make artsy websites, you first need to understand the nitty-gritties of code. Similarly, when learning anything, there are bound to be elements that you simply don't want to engage with. Here, the degree to which you care about your long-term goal will dictate how bearable this hard work will be. A method I routinely use to grind through such times is constantly reminding myself the following: nothing easy is ever worth doing because everyone else will just do it, thereby it dropping in value; ease goes up, supply goes up, value goes down.

Don't feed ignorance

One of the biggest roadblocks to learning is assuming something is wrong/irrelevant just because you don't understand it. We do this subconsciously all the time. I, for one, found myself guilty of it more often than I'd like to admit. As Dr Feynman said, 'The first principle is that you must not fool yourself and you are the easiest person to fool.'

This is definitely one of the more difficult problems to tackle in the pursuit of learning, and to be completely honest, I still haven't found any foolproof solutions to it. However, as a first step, I recommend learning about cognitive biases, logical fallacies and similar concepts.

This will help you gain clarity about your own personal blind-spots. Furthermore, when learning anything new, I consciously default to the assumption that I'm the one at fault whenever there is a discrepancy between what is being taught and what I'm being able to acquire. This practice helps uproot all the available information *before* coming to any conclusions.

A wise man once said, 'It is the mark of an educated mind to be able to entertain a thought without accepting it.'

Kill multitasking

Unlike what school promotes, learning several things simultaneously often leads to learning nothing at all. Pick one topic, and devote sufficient time and energy. As covered before, learning is like marination, it only happens over time. However, if you cannot restrict yourself to only one field, try to pick those that have clear relationships. This will leverage associative learning and greatly increase your capacity to retain information.

Moreover, get rid of any distractions!

The very act of switching from one activity to another—say, from reading a book to opening social media—requires energy. Over time, the constant switching from one activity to another, becomes a significant drain on your limited daily supply of brain power. Most importantly, these distractions steal from you your most valuable asset—time. They are specifically designed to do so! I'll let Sean Parker, the first president of Facebook, prove my point.

> The thought process that went into building these applications, Facebook being the first of them…was all about: 'How do we consume as much of your time and conscious attention as possible?'…And that means that we need to sort of give you a little dopamine hit every once in a while, because someone liked or commented on a photo or a post or whatever. And that's

going to get you to contribute more content, and that's going to get you…more likes and comments…It's a social-validation feedback loop… exactly the kind of thing that a hacker like myself would come up with, because you're exploiting a vulnerability in human psychology.[10]

Leverage Optimal Conditions

As covered before, you have a limited amount of energy per day. This makes the short time-period after a good night's sleep a unique opportunity to pursue effective learning; good sleep is critical. As the day proceeds, this window will inevitably close because the mere act of being alive and making decisions (what clothes to wear, where to eat, what to do, etc.) demands a LOT of energy. Of course, there are some activities—especially creative endeavours—that bear fruit arbitrarily, but learning is qualitatively different. It requires a greater level of conscious effort and decision-making, which makes the surplus energy incredibly potent. Use it.

Cultivate the muscle for delayed gratification

In the 1960s, a Stanford professor, Walter Mischel, began running a series of experiments we now refer to as the Marshmallow Test.[11] A simplified version of the study is as follows: for a group of a few hundred children aged 4-5, the researchers brought each into a room and proposed a deal: you may eat one marshmallow now, or wait for fifteen minutes and eat two. Unsurprisingly, most kids picked the first option. The interesting findings emerged when the researchers tracked each child's successes over time. In order to get a holistic measure of success, they tracked the children on a battery of metrics such as wealth, health, education and personal relationships. They gathered data for approximately forty years, and the results were eye-opening—on practically every measure, the small group of children who successfully waited for the second marshmallow significantly outperformed those who didn't.[12]

What does this tell us?

The ability to endure through short-term pain is a very good predictor of long-term success. Now, for many, this is not new information, but we never seem to integrate this rationale into our lives. I suspect this is because we haven't really understood what makes it true in the first place. So I will break it down for you.

You see, almost every activity can be broken into one of two categories: (1) those that provide instant gratification, and (2) those that provide delayed gratification. The first are activities such as eating fast food, engaging in social media, playing video games, etc.—generally, activities that provide pleasure *in the moment, but are net-negative in the long run.* And the second are activities such as physical exercise, eating healthy food, meditation, etc.—generally, activities that provide very little to no pleasure *in the moment, but are net-positive in the long run.* However, for each category, after they're completed, we swiftly revert to our baseline from the pleasure/difficulty we experience.

Now, here's where the magic happens. Over time, due to the method through which habits are formed, *the very act tends to be the cause for the activity to repeat itself.* Simply put, your brain remembers the cause-and-effect cycle—you engage with social media, you scroll through the feed or get likes, your brain releases dopamine and so, it remembers the connection between social media and feeling good. This phenomenon is what makes activities a net-negative or net-positive in the long run. The more you do something, the more likely you are to continue with it.

Extrapolating on this, the more you practice an activity, the more you will notice your brain relying on activities of similitude to attain a good feeling. This is due to second-order consequences—in other words, the domino effect. When we perform an action, there is an effect, which then becomes the action for another effect, and this cycle perpetuates. This significantly increases the potential net-gain/loss over time of one single activity that might not seem like much at the moment. Let me illustrate by example:

> You eat healthy → You continue to eat healthy → Other net-positive habits form (for example, sleeping well) → Brain receives quality energy → Emotions are more stable → Work quality improves → You achieve financial stability → Personal life improves → etc.

Most people don't look past the immediate consequence of an action, and end up making decisions based on heavily skewed information. Sure, when buying that PlayStation you're going to see the effects in your bank statement, but what you're not going to see is the opportunity cost incurred by the many hours spent actually using it, and the infinite series of events that could've manifested if you otherwise spent that time productively. We can boil this entire series of phenomena down to the following graph.

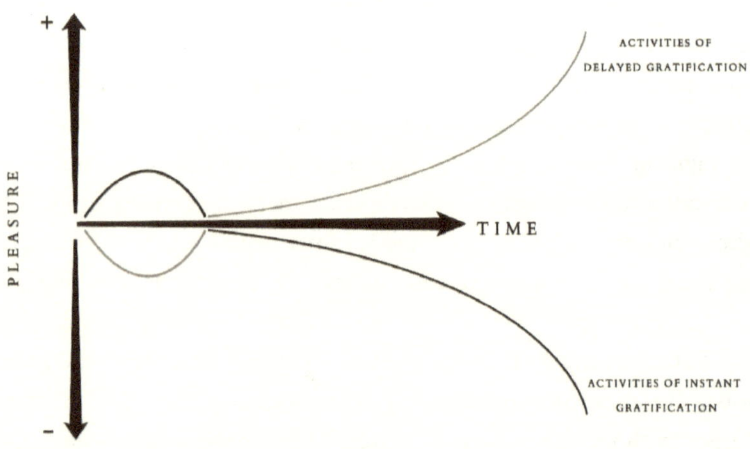

Why is all this relevant to learning? Well, learning is the quintessential example of delayed gratification. It is a low-dopamine activity. Thus, to effectively learn, we must overcome the trap of instant gratification. So, the natural next question becomes, how do we do that?

Many view people who easily seem to delay gratification as strange and assume they naturally don't enjoy what the masses get distracted by. This is far from the truth. Fast food, social media, videogames, and the whole panoply is highly addictive for everyone. The concept, at least based on my findings, that must be understood is *acquired taste*. Simply put, it is a attraction towards something that people tend to dislike if they haven't had substantial exposure to it. In other words, the more you do something, the more likely you are to enjoy it, or at least, not dislike it as much. It's very much like alcohol or coffee—as kids, the taste is horrible, but as we grow older and the more we consume them (for the effects, of course), the more they become bearable. Similarly, every successful person has leveraged this concept to acquire the taste of activities that provide delayed gratification.

Moreover, if out of the blue, you decide to learn, chances are you're not going to enjoy it. Your lifestyle—one ridden with social media, fast food, sugar, parties, Netflix, videogames, etc.—has completely desensitized you to dopamine. The same way an alcohol or caffeine-tolerance works, you're going to need an increasing amount of dopamine to get an equivalent feeling of pleasure. Here, learning won't stand a chance at being accomplished in a sustainable manner, because before you know it, your mind will wander in a single-minded pursuit to attain dopamine. I'll say it again, learning is a low-dopamine activity. Natural production of this chemical exists as a means to motivate us, but when we normalize an artificially high amount, we sacrifice our ability to be motivated to do anything but activities that give us mass dopamine. In this situation, you have little hope of succeeding.

The key takeaway here is that anyone can cultivate the ability to delay gratification; and knowing you can do it is essential to be able to do it. Yes, the initial phase is tough, but the following methods can help you get through it:

1) Dopamine detox: cut out as many dopamine-releasing activities as you can afford to for a period of time. This will reduce your tolerance and enable you to enjoy low-dopamine activities. Understand dopamine and control it; don't let it control you.
   a) Start small and then work your way up. Make it so easy that you feel ashamed of yourself if you don't do it.
2) If you skipped Step 1, go back and do it. Strengthening your body and mind is vital.
3) Meditation—even 5-20 minutes a day—will help. Before indulging in instantly gratifying activities, we often have thoughts such as, 'I deserve this' and similar nonsense. Meditation allows you to call yourself out on all the BS in your thought process.
4) Set accountability mechanisms.

In sum, cultivating the habit to delay gratification will give you more of a disproportionate advantage than any secret anyone claims to know. This isn't an apocryphal sentiment of older generations towards us who've never experienced real hardship (wars, famines, etc.). These are bare necessities to not only sustainably achieve the life we all dream about, but also avoid an amazing amount of self-imposed misery, which seems to be ubiquitous in a generation that has, ironically, been born in an objectively better time than everything that has come before.

Step 3: Brighten your flashlight

Did you ever play any of the classic Pokémon games? *Fire Red, Leaf Green* and the other OGs? If so, remember entering those caves where you couldn't see anything? And you had to just roam around and work your way to clarity through trial and error. Well, the path to learning is exactly like that! For the non-video game geeks, think about it like this: learning a new field of knowledge is like walking into a pitch-black cave with only a flashlight. And the path to successful learning is nothing but walking around based on your best guess, repeatedly bumping into the walls, by doing which you eventually get an idea of what and where everything is.

(*Rock Tunnel from Pokémon: FireRed*)

In other words, the flashlight is your mind—specifically, the sum total of the pre-existing knowledge you possess. It is the only source of clarity you have while navigating through uncharted territories, such as learning something new. Now, obviously, the quantity of knowledge is less important than quality. But as a general rule of thumb, assuming good quality, the broader your foundational knowledge base, the better you will be able to learn anything.

So, how can you brighten your flashlight? Well, go get a general education!

And please, I don't mean those offered by traditional colleges. As we covered before, they're simply unable to provide the relevant information we need. And even in the off-chance they do so, they make it a class you have to pass, making it a pursuit to get the grade than actually learn the material.

Instead, I suggest you find better sources, especially those that are cheaper and more time-efficient. If you don't want to pay a dime, no worries, books and the internet have you covered. I'm not even exaggerating when I say more than half of my knowledge is due to the internet. The only catch here is that you're going to have to not only figure out what you need to learn but also filter through an ocean of nonsense.

Step 4: Identify the destination/Focus on the questions, not the answers

In school, we're told no question is a stupid question. Even the brilliance of the late Carl Sagan had this to say:

> There are naive questions, tedious questions, ill-phrased questions, questions put after inadequate self-criticism. But every question is a cry to understand the world. There is no such thing as a dumb question.[13]

The essence of such statements exists to remind us to never stop seeking knowledge, and that the quest to attain answers requires failure. To not ask any questions at all is a sure-fire strategy to remain ignorant. But, as Dr Sagan alludes, assuming a sincere intent to understand, there are god-awful questions, okay questions, good questions and eye-opening questions. This is because it is the quality of the question that determines the quality of the answer. You can ask, 'Is the earth flat?' From where we stand, it certainly looks that way (hence the flat-earthers). Or, you can ask, 'If it weren't flat—let's say, if it were spherical—how would it look?' The difference is subtle but significant. Furthermore, it is the question that determines the direction you move in, and the method by which you do so. It is the tool we use to attain truth. Use subpar tools and you will only find subpar answers. One of the hallmarks of a good question is the ease with which it provides you with an answer. Einstein said it best:

> If I had an hour to solve a problem, I'd spend fifty-five minutes thinking about the problem and five minutes thinking about solutions.

So, coming back to your journey to self-educate, the first question should always be, 'What do I want to do, that I cannot do right now?' Or, 'Why am I learning this?'

Be as clear and specific as you can.

Once you're aware of your true intentions, then you may ask, 'What do I need to learn to accomplish this goal?' This is your destination. You must identify your destination *before* you begin your learning journey. It is vital.

All along, never forget the utility and power of the well-crafted question. After all, thinking is nothing but a never-ending series of questions you ask and answer yourself. So, the better you get at asking questions, the better you get at thinking. I do not need to emphasize the importance of thinking better.

Step 5: The map

After you're crystal clear on what your final destination is, you must now figure out how to get there. Think of it like a treasure map. In the previous step, you identified where X marks the spot. Now you must work backward to your current position. This gives you a concrete path to follow, without which finding the treasure is highly unlikely.

How does one make the treasure map? To do this, we seek guidance from first principles. You see, there are two predominant methods of thinking we use in everyday life: (1) Reasoning by first principles—the process by which you draw conclusions based on the fundamental building blocks of an idea. (2) Reasoning by analogy—the process by which you draw conclusions based on widely held beliefs present in society.

Both have their place in the world, but when it comes to innovating, optimizing, teaching or learning, the former is superior by a significant margin. In fact, the latter is one of the reasons why college has ended up being more of a burden than an opportunity for growth. Everybody is taking student loans, so it must be the best path. Classic reasoning by analogy.

Essentially, your map is a hierarchy of building blocks. At the top, you have your destination, and at the bottom, you have the simple parts that add up to make the whole. For example, think about how we teach language to children. So, if the destination is a language, we can break a message into sentences, sentences into words, and words into letters. We can't break letters down any further, therefore we have arrived at the first principle. This is why we begin here.

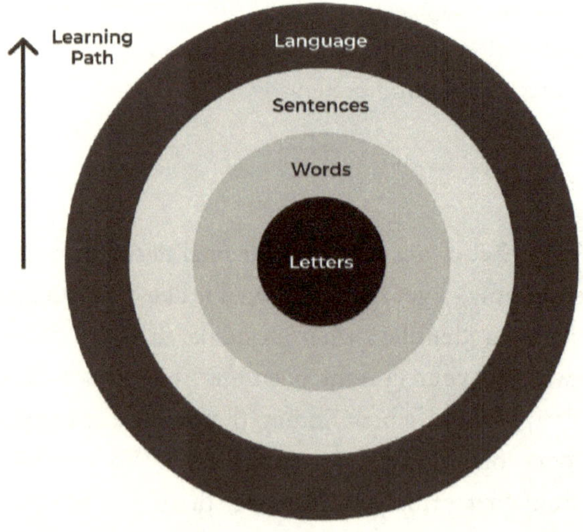

To create your map, I recommend immersing yourself in the subject you're trying to learn. Online videos are a great place to start—they're definitely my go-to at this stage—but how you choose to attain information is a matter of personal preference. Of course, try to search for material suitable for beginners, but don't ignore something just because you don't understand it. Assuming you're starting from zero, almost anything you are exposed to at this point will be a net positive. Completely immersing yourself in a subject will quickly enable you to identify the concepts and skills needed to achieve your end goal. Remember, at this stage the goal is not to learn, but to figure out what to learn.

Step 6: The source > information

After creating your map, don't jump right into absorbing anything and everything. You won't be able to ascertain what's true, relevant, expired, etc. Moreover, each source of information will assume a different set of prerequisites when providing information; making the learning process unnecessarily lengthy. Therefore, it is wise to spend the time identifying a handful of authority figures on a subject, and then learn only from them, at least in the initial stages. Now, to actually do this is pretty tough. We don't really have a robust and accessible solution to filtering out the good sources of information from the bad. This is one of the great bottlenecks of learning we still have to overcome. For now, I'll leave you with my common practices:

1) Identify who you admire in the field.
2) Check reviews, testimonials, comments, etc. The more successful the person recommending it is, the better.
3) Verify their history—has the source practiced what they preach?
4) Cut losses. You often don't realize that the source is not worth

your time until much later. When you do, don't hesitate—move on.

That said, learning has never been easier. Today, no knowledge is restricted by the boundaries of institutions. All of K-12 material can be found on Khan Academy, and the same information taught at the most elite schools can be found on websites such as Edx, for free. This, coupled with the immense amount of knowledge freely available on YouTube, is jaw-dropping in its own right. We've come to associate YouTube with mindless videos, but the truth is that it has evolved into something better described as an autodidact's oasis. Passionate teachers creating content, gold nuggets from successful CEOs, TED talks, and intellectual debates between celebrities of academia, are just a few examples of what YouTube has to offer.

Apart from the internet, we have another incredible resource. In today's day and age, books are an undervalued asset. I'm most definitely not a preacher of recreational reading; that is a daft argument to make in a world with multisensory media. However, when it comes to learning, there are very few other resources with equivalent efficacy.

As recently as a couple of years ago, I used to think people trying to convince me to read were only doing so because they were from previous generations and didn't understand the tremendous value of the internet. Truth is, I didn't understand books. For one, many who write books are those who have done very well in life—these are the people you want to learn from. For them, time is the most valuable asset, which makes condensing a lifetime of learning in 200 pages the most time-efficient option. Moreover, the most important and powerful concepts—concepts that you want to learn—tend to be abstract and complex in nature. Thus, long-form media remains the only means through which such information can be passed on in a concrete manner. Lastly, the act of reading requires time, and time allows the material to marinate in your brain. It becomes an active process as opposed to a passive one, like watching a video. Not to mention, the more you read, the faster you get at it, and the more efficiently you can learn.

Step 7: Be the spongiest sponge

Now, finally, learning begins. Most people jump right to this step and then wonder why they're having such a hard time. After you've got your sources down, absorb *everything* they have to offer, according to your map. Be relentless in your pursuit.

Step 8: Execute

After an adequate time spent absorbing information, you must put it into action. This step may look different according to the nature of the material being learned. Nonetheless, the act of practicing what you've absorbed is key.

Step 9: Reflect

This is as important a step as any other. We all tend to overlook it, remarking that it makes no difference, is boring, or a whole host of waterless excuses. By doing so, we severely handicap our ability to learn. To overcome this obstacle, here's what you can do: after you implement what you've absorbed, there are going to be things that worked, and things that didn't. You must take the time to explicitly have a conversation with yourself about why you think what happened, happened. You may ponder on questions such as, 'Why did I fail where I did? Why did I succeed where I did? Where were my weaknesses?'

Step 10: Go to Step 7

Soak it all up

I acknowledge that some may find the process incredibly difficult to execute in its entirety. That's okay, we all routinely fall short somewhere or the other. Perfection is a great goal, not an achievable one. However, the more accurately you can execute the processes, the faster and better you will learn. That is guaranteed.

Furthermore, some might ignore or not even comprehend what they've read. That is okay too. I know that if someone told me all this when I was eighteen I would've probably still continued doing what I believed was correct. Nevertheless, looking back, I do wish someone had introduced me to these concepts in a structured manner. Because, sooner or later, you will see the value in it. When that happens, you will not only know exactly what to do, but also have a reference point, instead of having to figure it all out on your own.

Epilogue

If it's not clear already, I am an advocate of formal education. But I am also an advocate for the prosperity of civilization. And as it stands, the two seem destined to be incompatible. Just as our philosophy of truth kept the fruits of science at bay for more than 99% of human existence, our philosophy of education is doing the same to collective competence.

Consequently, our perception of reality has gotten so convoluted that we've lost awareness of the truths that have allowed us, humans, to get to where we are. As mentioned before, understanding is the superpower that facilitated our dominance on earth. But now, ironically, we've created a world far too complex for the common Homo sapien to understand in a manner sufficient to adequately direct themselves in life. Now, reducing the world's complexity is neither what I'm arguing for nor the cause of the issue. It is our inability to proportionally match the complexity with an effective system of knowledge dissemination that has led most to be unaware of their extraordinary capacity to understand. Our superpower—your superpower—is being taken away, and we're just letting it happen.

The kicker is that our willingness to learn is so innate that it can never be eradicated in its entirety, but it most certainly has been systematically subdued in the millions. This is a problem. For many years, our society has trodden along because the obstacles that once stood were not those that were amplified by the inadequacies of our education system. But now, as Yuval Harari has succinctly put, 'The top 3 issues our civilization faces are Technological Disruption,

Climate Change, and Nuclear Disaster.' In other words, they are global problems; *no one country can solve them*. Vital to solving any is mass cooperation at a degree greater than ever before. And I must emphasize, a prerequisite for cooperating societies are competent societies—*not only* competent individuals. Put another way, if a minority percentage of the population chose to turn a blind eye to competency, society could still progress. Now, unfortunately, this is not the case.

Best exemplified by our system of government. In a democracy, competence is no determinant of an individual's power to put another in office. Thus, the fate of a nation resides with the sum-competence, if you will, of its people. For many years, demagogues and such have exploited this very fundamental weakness of democracy. When ultimate power resides with the people, Pathos becomes our Achilles heel.

Therefore, if you take away anything from this book, let it be this: For too long now our education system has perpetuated itself. It has done great good, I concede. But now, change is not a mere nice-to-have, it's an absolute necessity. If we don't, maybe you or I won't bear the brunt, but our kids most certainly will. In my eyes, even though the problem is monumental, the first line of attack is far from inconceivable. Why not make a serious effort at making learning fun? Let's leverage Pathos to our advantage. For the love of God, this does not mean gamification and other such nonsense our institutes seem to pursue in the name of improvement. What I mean is to kindle a child's innate curiosity; for if curiosity is realized, every instance of new understanding provides a natural physical high. Nature's way of making the difficult task of learning fun.

For schools, a good place to begin this transformation is by acknowledging all that was mentioned over the course of the preceding chapters. Today, you employ a very backward philosophy to develop competency. Instead of making kids want to learn, you enforce the act of learning. Inadvertently, not only does this work in favour of a minority, which, as just discussed, is no longer tolerable; but also, is where stems a blatant misrepresentation of the world. And the kids, who know no better, conform to their detriment. We must, as the saying goes,

> Prepare the child for the road, not the road for the child.

In all honesty, I don't expect change to come from within. This phenomenon of existing institutions perpetuating themselves is not a new one. People will take matters into their own hands (as they already have), and the lack of initiative by the incumbents will be the cause of their downfall. It is only a matter of time.

With this, we come to the end of this book. I hope you found it useful. Thank you for your time and I wish you the best for all your future endeavours.

Sincerely,
Sid Sanghvi

Acknowledgments

Over two arduous years, there have been many who have contributed to the realization of this project. I shall not try to name them all as the effort may expose my far-from-ideal memory. But let that not undermine the deep sense of gratitude I wish to express to each person on this journey. Thank you.

However, I must state the following: Dad, Mom, I certainly would not have reached this far without your love and support. Words cannot express how much I appreciate everything you both have done for me, so I hope my actions will.

Notes & References

Prologue

1. Nagdy, Mohamed, and Max Roser. '*Intelligence.*' Our World in Data, 14 July 2015, ourworldindata.org/intelligence. Accessed: May 2018

Chapter 2

1. Khan Academy, Sal Khan, '*Origins of life*', www.khanacademy.org/science/ biology/history-of-life-on-earth/history-life-on-earth/v/origins-of-life, accessed Feb 2019.
2. Harari, Yuval N. *Sapiens: A Brief History of Humankind*. Harper, 2015.
3. Web Library, Encyclopedia Britannica, '*Human Evolution*', www. britannica.com/science/human-evolution, accessed March 2019.
4. Ridley, M. (2003). Nature via nurture: Genes, experience, and what makes us human. New York: HarperCollins. See also: Konner, M. (2002). The tangled wing: Biological constraints on the human spirit, 2nd ed. New York: Holt.
5. Malcolm Knowles, *The Adult Learner*, 5th ed. (Woburn, MA: Butterworth-Heinemann, 1998 [originally published 1973]).
6. Kandel, Eric R. *In Search of Memory - the Emergence of a New Science of Mind*. W W Norton & Co Ltd, 2007.
7. Gray, Peter. *Free to Learn: Why Unleashing the Instinct to Play Will Make Our Children Happier, More Self-Reliant, and Better Students for Life*. Basic Books, 2015.
8. See index 4.
9. See index 7.

Chapter 3

1. Salamone, F. A. (1997). The Yanomami and their interpreters: Fierce people or fierce interpreters? Lanham, MD: University Press of America.

2. Woodburn, J. (1968). An introduction to Hazda ecology. In R. Lee & I. DeVore (Eds.), Man the hunter. Chicago: Aldine. See also: Draper, P. (1988). Technological change and child behavior among the !Kung. Ethnology, 27, 339—365. See also: Bock, J., & Johnson, S. E. (2004). Subsistence ecology and play among the Okavango Delta peoples of Botswana. Human Nature, 15, 63—81.

3. Barry, H., Child, I., Bacon, M. K. (1959). The relation of child training to subsistence economy. American Anthropologist, 61, 51—63.

Chapter 4

1. Gray, Peter. *Free to Learn: Why Unleashing the Instinct to Play Will Make Our Children Happier, More Self-Reliant, and Better Students for Life.* Chapter 3. Basic Books, 2015

2. Orme, N. (2001), *Medieval children*, p 315. New Haven, CT: Yale University Press.

3. Ensign, F. C. (1921). *Compulsory school attendance and child labor.* Iowa City, Iowa: Athens Press.

Chapter 5

1. Gray, Peter. *Free to Learn: Why Unleashing the Instinct to Play Will Make Our Children Happier, More Self-Reliant, and Better Students for Life.* Chapter 3. Basic Books, 2015

2. Mulhern, J. (1959). *A history of education: A social interpretation,* 2nd ed. New York: Ronald Press. P. 383. See also: index 1.

3. See index 1. See also: Melton, J. V. H. (1988). *Absolutism and the eighteenth-century origins of compulsory schooling in Prussia and Austria.* Cambridge: Cambridge University Press

4. See index 2.

Chapter 6

1. Salman Khan, Michael Noer. *The History of Education.* Published November 1st 2012. https://www.youtube.com/watch?v=LqTwDDTj b6g&list=PLn3PCgQYd60llwuXbXrwDmvQsppbUlNmX&index=3&t =0s. Accessed Sept 30th, 2019

2. Ensign, F. C. (1921). *Compulsory school attendance and child labor.* Iowa City, Iowa: Athens Press

3. See index 1.

4. Brendan Conway-Smith and Eve Zarifa. *The Origins of the American Public Education System: Horace Mann & the Prussian Model of Obedience.* Sept 30th, 2019 http://farmwars.info/?p=11960

5. Heywood, C. (2001). *A history of childhood: Children and childhood in the West from medieval to modern times.* Oxford: Blackwell

6. See index 4.

7. Addresses to the German Nation (1807), Second Address : 'The General Nature of the New Education'. Chicago and London, The Open Court Publishing Company, 1922, p. 21

8. The Impact of Science on Society (1952), SCIENTIFIC TECHNIQUE IN OLIGARCHY. NEW YORK, AMS PRESS, 1968, p. 50.

Chapter 7

1. Taleb, Nassim Nicholas. Antifragile: Things That Gain from Disorder. Random House, 2016.

Chapter 9

1. Rampell, C. (2009, August 27). SAT scores and family income. *Economix* (blog). The New York Times. http://economix.blogs.nytimes. com/2009/08/27/sat-scores-and-family-income

2. Cooper, Harris, Barbara Nye, Kelly Charlton, James Lindsay, and Scott Greathouse. 1996. 'The Effects of Summer Vacation on Achievement Test Scores: A Narrative and Meta-Analytic Review.' Review of Educational Research 66 (3): 227—68.

3. Jacob, Brian, Lars Lefgren, and David Sims. 2010. 'The Persistence of Teacher-Induced Learning.' Journal of Human Resources 45 (4): 915—43. See also: Cascio, Elizabeth, and Douglas Staiger. 2012. 'Knowledge, Tests, and Fadeout in Educational Interventions.' NBER Working Paper No. 18038. http://www.nber.org/papers/w18038.

4. Einstein, A. (1949). Autobiography. In P. Schilpp, Albert Einstein: Philosopher-scientist. Evanston, IL: Library of Living Philosophers.

5. See index 4.

6. Sandra L. Hofferth and John F. Sandberg, 'How American Children Spend Their Time,' *Journal of Marriage and Family* 63, no. 2 (May 2001)

7. Bruni, F. (2016, January 19). Rethinking college admissions. The New York Times. Retrieved from https://www.nytimes.com/2016/01/20/opinion/rethinking-college-admissions.html. See also: Rosin, H. (2015, November 20). The Silicon Valley suicides. The Atlantic. Retrieved from https://www.theatlantic.com/magazine/archive/2015/12/the-silicon-valley-suicides/413140. See also: Spencer, K. (2017, April 5). It takes a suburb: A town struggles to ease student stress. The New York Times. Retrieved from https://www.nytimes.com/2017/04/05/education/edlife/overachievers-student-stress-in-high-school-.html?_r=0

8. McMahon, R. (2007). Everybody does it: Academic cheating is at an all time high. *San Francisco Chronicle*, September 9. See also: Oleck, J. (2008). Most high school students admit to cheating. *School Library Journal*, March 10. See also: Pytel, B. (2007). Cheating is on the rise. Published online at www.suite101.com/content/cheating-is-on-the-rise-a31238.

9. Big Picture Learning. https://www.bigpicture.org/apps/pages/international.

Chapter 12

1. Cappelli, Peter. *Will College Pay off?: a Guide to the Most Important Financial Decision You'll Ever Make.* PublicAffairs, 2015.

2. Shorts and Faces: Ivory Hunting on the Charles,' Fortune 37 (January 1948): 116.

3. 'Ch 9: Less like a Yacht.' The End of College: Creating the Future of Learning and the University of Everywhere, by Kevin Carey, Riverhead Books, 2016.

4. Fang, Hanming, and Andrea Moro. 2011. 'Theories of Statistical Discrimination and Affirmitave Action: A Survey.' In *Handbook of Social Economics*, vol 1A, edited by Jess Benhabib, Matthew jacksn, and Albert Bisin, 133-200. Amsterdam: Elsevier

5. The Steve Jobs 95 Interview unabridged. https://www.youtube.com/watch?v=M6Oxl5dAnR0

6. Ashley Thorne. *College Tuition vs. Home Prices vs. CPI...No Comment.* https://www.nas.org/blogs/article/college_tuition_vs_home_prices_vs_cpi_no_comment

7. Bloomberg. Labor Department. Ilan Kolet. *College Tuition's 1,120 Percent Increase.* https://www.bloomberg.com/news/articles/2012-08-23/college-tuitions-1-120-percent-increase

8. Camilo Maldonado. Jul 24, 2018. *Price Of College Increasing Almost 8 Times Faster Than Wages.* https://www.forbes.com/sites/camilomaldonado/2018/07/24/price-of-college-increasing-almost-8-times-faster-than-wages/#665532e66c1d

9. The College Board, *Annual Survey of Colleges* (Princeton, NJ: 2014)

Chapter 13

1. Mascaro O., Csibra G. (2012). *Representation of stable social dominance relations by human infants.* Proc. Natl. Acad. Sci. U.S.A. 109, 6862—6867. 10.1073/pnas.1113194109. https://www.ncbi.nlm.nih.gov/pmc/articles/PMC4469834/

2. US News & World Report. Robert Morse, Eric Brooks, Matt Mason. Sept 8 2019. https://www.usnews.com/education/best-colleges/articles/how-us-news-calculated-the-rankings. See also: https://www.usnews.com/education/best-colleges/articles/ranking-criteria-and-weights

3. Burnsed, B. (2015, September 18). Athletics departments that make more than they spend still a minority. National Collegiate Athletic Association. http://ncaa.org/about/resources/media-center/news/

athletics-departments-that-make-more-than-they-spend-still-minority

4. 'Ch 3: The Absolut Rolex Plan.' *The End of College: Creating the Future of Learning and the University of Everywhere*, by Kevin Carey, Riverhead Books, 2016

5. Daniel Luzer. 'The Prestige Racket,' Washington Monthly, August 22, 2010.

6. Associated, The (1988-08-07). '7% Rise Reported in College Tuition for 1988-89'. New York Times. Retrieved 2014-01-18

7. Tom Van Riper, 'Most Expensive Colleges in America,' Forbes, January 19, 2007

8. See index 4.

9. See index 4.

10. Jay P. Greene, 'Administrative Bloat at American Universities: The Real Reason for High Costs in Higher Education,' Goldwater Institute Policy Report, no. 239, August 17, 2010, 1, https://goldwaterinstitute.org/article/administrative-bloat-at-american-universities-the/

11. National Center for Education Statistics. (2011). Fall staff in postsecondary institutions, *Digest of Education Statistics, & IPEDS Human resources Survey 2011-2012*. Washington, DC: U.S. Department of Education, Institute of Educations Sciences. http://www.aaup.org/sites/default/files/files/2014%20salary%20report/Figure%201.pdf

12. Kerr, C. (1963). The uses of the university. Cambridge, MA: Harvard University Press.

13. Marcus, J. (2016, October 6). The reason behind colleges' ballooning bureaucracies. The Atlantic. Retrieved from https://www.theatlantic.com/education/archive/2016/10/ballooning-bureaucracies-shrinking-checkbooks/503066

14. Braswell, S. (2016, April 24). The fightin' administrators: The birth of a college bureaucracy. Point Taken. Retrieved from http://www.pbs.org/wgbh/point-taken/blog/ozy-fightin-administrators-birth-college-bureaucracy. See also: Christensen, K. (2015, October 17). Is UC spending too little on teaching, too much on administration? Los Angeles Times. Retrieved from http://www.latimes.com/local/education/la-me-uc-spending-20151011-story.html

15. See, for example, Catropa, D., & Andrews, M. (2013, February 8). Bemoaning the corporatization of higher education. Inside Higher Ed. Retrieved from https://www.insidehighered.com/blogs/stratedgy/bemoaning-corporatization-higher-education

16. Catropa & Andrews (2013); see n. 15. See also: Lewis (2007), pp. 4—5. See also: McArdle, M. (2015, August 13). Sheltered students go to college, avoid education. Bloomberg View. Retrieved from https://www.bloomberg.com/view/articles/2015-08-13/sheltered-students-go-to-college-avoid-education

17. Author's calculation from IPEDS data. 'Ch 12: Your Children and the University of Everywhere.' *The End of College: Creating the Future of Learning and the University of Everywhere*, by Kevin Carey, Riverhead Books, 2016

18. Attewell, Paul, David Lavin, Thurston Domina, and Tania Levey. 2006. 'New Evidence on College Remediation.' Journal of Higher Education 77 (5): 886—924.

19. See Institute of Education Sciences, National Center for Education Statistics, 'First-Year Undergraduate Remedial Coursetaking: 1999—2000, 2003—04, 2007—08,' Statistics in Brief, January 2013. Sixteen percent of four-year students in private colleges took remedial courses in 2000, versus 15 percent in 2008, almost no change.

20. 'Chapter 1: Why Do People with More Education Get Better Jobs?' *Will College Pay off?: a Guide to the Most Important Financial Decision You'll Ever Make*, by Peter Cappelli, PublicAffairs, 2015

21. Center on Budget and Policy Priorities. *MICHAEL MITCHELL, MICHAEL LEACHMAN, AND KATHLEEN MASTERSON. A Lost Decade in Higher Education Funding. AUGUST 23, 2017.* https://www.cbpp.org/research/state-budget-and-tax/a-lost-decade-in-higher-education-funding

Chapter 14

1. Naughton, K. (2017, October). Speaking freely—What students think about expression at American colleges. FIRE. Retrieved from https://www.thefire.org/publications/student-attitudes-free-speech-survey

2. Columbia College. (n.d.). The Core curriculum: Literature Humanities. Retrieved from https://www.college.columbia.edu/core/lithum

3. Johnson, K., Lynch, T., Monroe, E., & Wang, T. (2015, April 30). Our identities matter in Core classrooms. *Columbia Daily Spectator*. Retrieved from http://spc.columbiaspectator.com/opinion/2015/04/30/our-identities-matter-core-classrooms [inactive]

4. For extensive analyses of survey data showing that the campus dynamic related to speech has changed in the last few years, see Stevens, S., & Haidt, J. (2018, April 11), The skeptics are wrong part 2: Speech culture on campus is changing. Retrieved from https://heterodoxacademy.org/the-skeptics-are-wrong-part-2

5. Barrett, K. (2016, September 22). Walking on eggshells—How political correctness is changing the campus dynamic. The Sophian. Retrieved from http://www.thesmithsophian.com/walking-on-eggshells-how-political-correctness-is-changing-the-campus-dynamics

6. Friedersdorf, C. (2017, May 8). The destructiveness of call-out culture on campus. The Atlantic. Retrieved from https://www.theatlantic.com/politics/archive/2017/05/call-out-culture-is-stressing-out-college-students/524679

7. Haidt, J. (2017, April 26). Intimidation is the new normal on campus. The Chronicle of Higher Education. Retrieved from https://www.chronicle.com/article/Intimidation-Is-the-New-Normal/239890

8. Higher Education Research Institute (For more about the HERI survey, visit https://heri.ucla.edu). Data is from nationally representative surveys of professors in the United States. Graphed by Sam Abrams.

9. See analysis of all relevant studies prior to 2014 in: Duarte, J. L., Crawford, J. T., Stern, C., Haidt, J., Jussim, L., & Tetlock, P. E. (2015). Political diversity will improve social psychological science. Behavioral and Brain Sciences, 38, 1—13. For the most recent data point, seventeen to one, see: Langbert, M., Quain, A. J., & Klein, D. B. (2016). Faculty voter registration in economics, history, journalism, law, and psychology. Econ Journal Watch, 13(3), 422—451.

10. Lukianff G., Haidt J., (2018). *The Coddling of the American Mind*. Part 2 - Chapter 5: Witch Hunts (Penguin Press: New York)

11. Bauer-Wolf, J. (2017, October 6). Free speech advocate silenced. Inside Higher Ed. Retrieved from https://www.insidehighered.com/news/2017/10/06/william-mary-students-who-shut-down-aclu-event-broke-conduct-code

12. Rioters break windows, set fire to force cancellation of Breitbart editor's UC—Berkeley talk. (2017, February 1). Fox News. Retrieved from http://www.foxnews.com/us/2017/02/01/rioters-break-windows-set-fire-to-force-cancellation-breitbart-editors-uc-berkeley-talk.html. See also: RTQuestionsMore (Producer). (2017, February 1). Kiara Robles talks to RT International [Video file]. Retrieved from https://www.youtube.com/watch?v=SUQdlc8Gc-g&feature=youtu.be. See also: Lukianff G., Haidt J., (2018). *The Coddling of the American Mind.* Part 2: Chapter 4 - Intimidation and Violence. (Penguin Press: New York). See also: Fabian, P. (Producer).(2017, February 2). Protestors beating people at Milo Yiannopoulos event @ U.C. Berkeley [Video file]. Retrieved from https://www.youtube.com/watch?v=GSMKGRyWKas.

13. The demonstrators caused an estimated $100,000 in damage on campus, the university said, and an additional $400,000 to $500,000 elsewhere, according to Downtown Berkeley Association CEO John Caner.' Kutner, M. (2017, February 1). Inside the black bloc protest strategy that shut down Berkeley. Newsweek. Retrieved from http://www.newsweek.com/2017/02/24/berkeley-protest-milo-yiannopoulos-black-bloc-556264.html

14. Cohen, R. (2017, February 7). What might Mario Savio have said about the Milo protest at Berkeley? The Nation. Retrieved from https://www.thenation.com/article/what-might-mario-savio-have-said-about-the-milo-protest-at-berkeley. See also: Ashenmiller, J. (2013). Mario Savio. Encyclopaedia Britannica Online. Retrieved from https://www.britannica.com/biography/Mario-Savio

15. Gross, N. (2016, September 30). Is there a 'Ferguson Effect'? The New York Times. Retrieved from https://www.nytimes.com/2016/10/02/opinion/sunday/is-there-a-ferguson-effect.html

16. Blume, H. (2017, April 9). Protesters disrupt talk by pro-police author, sparking free-speech debate at Claremont McKenna College. Los Angeles

Times. Retrieved from http://www.latimes.com/local/lanow/la-me-ln-macdonald-claremont-speech-disrupted-20170408-story.html. See also: Wootson, C. R., Jr. (2017, April 10). She wanted to criticize Black Lives Matter in a college speech. A protest shuts her down. The Washington Post. Retrieved from https://www.washingtonpost.com/news/grade-point/wp/2017/04/10/she-wanted-to-criticize-black-lives-matter-in-a-college-speech-a-protest-shut-her-down

17. Lukianff G., Haidt J., (2018). *The Coddling of the American Mind*. Part 1– Chapter 2: The Untruth of Emotional Reasoning (Penguin Press: New York)

18. *Disinvitation Database*. FIRE. Accessed: April 20th 2020. https://www.thefire.org/resources/disinvitation-database

19. Gray, H. H. (2012). *Searching for utopia: Universities and their histories.* Berkeley: University of California Press. p. 86

20. *Jordan Peterson debate on the gender pay gap, campus protests and postmodernism.* Channel 4 News. Youtube. Jan 16th 2018. https://www.youtube.com/watch?v=aMcjxSThD54

21. Good Life by Zhu. Generation Why. Song lyrics. https://genius.com/Zhu-good-life-lyrics

22. Solzhenitsyn, A. I. (1975). *The Gulag Archipelago, 1918—1956: An experiment in literary investigation* (Vol. 2) (T. P. Whitney, Trans.) New York, NY: Harper Perennial

23. 'WATCH: The House Financial Services Committee holds a hearing on the student loan crisis', Streamed live on Sep 10, 2019. *Youtube.* https://www.youtube.com/watch?v=9IKaKKZWp8E

24. MK Consulting (2015, December). Who graduates with excessive loan debt? www.studentaidpolicy.com/exccessive-debt

25. Institute for College Access and Success. (2016). Student debt and the class of 2015. http://ticas.org/sites/default/files/pub_files/classof2015.pdf

26. Pew Research, 'A Record One-in-Five Households Now Owe Student Loan Debt' September 26 2012, https://www.pewsocialtrends.org/2012/09/26/a-record-one-in-five-households-now-owe-student-loan-debt/

27. WATCH: The House Financial Services Committee holds a hearing on

the student loan crisis', Streamed live on Sep 10, 2019. *Youtube*. https://www.youtube.com/watch?v=9IKaKKZWp8E

28. James Pethokoukis, 'Why student loans might be the next recipient of a taxpayer bailout' AEIdeas (blog), November 28 2012, https://www.aei.org/education/higher-education/why-student-loans-might-be-the-next-recipient-of-a-taxpayer-bailout/

29. Jonathan Liand, 'What a Drag!' *Barron's*, April 16 2012. https://www.barrons.com/articles/SB500014240531119048574045773338426374 59600

30. The current level of student debt is keeping down house buying for this generation. Neil Irwin, 'How Student Debt May Be Stunting the Economy,' New York Times, May 14, 2014.

31. Paul J. DiMaggio and Walter W. Powell, 'The Iron Cage Revisited: Institutional Isomorphism and Collective Rationality in Organizational Fields,' *American Sociological Review* 48:2 (1983), pp. 147—60.

32. 'Ch 9: Less like a Yacht.' *The End of College: Creating the Future of Learning and the University of Everywhere*, by Kevin Carey, Riverhead Books, 2016. See also: Harvard University. https://www.harvard.edu/about-harvard/harvard-glance/history-presidency/henry-dunster

33. Charles W. Eliot, 'The New Education,' Atlantic Monthly, February 27, 1869

34. 'Chapter 2: A Sham, a Bauble, a Dodge.' *The End of College: Creating the Future of Learning and the University of Everywhere*, by Kevin Carey, Riverhead Books, 2016.

35. William James. '*The Ph.D. Octopus*' Harvard Monthly of March 1903. https://www.uky.edu/~eushe2/Pajares/octopus.html

36. Barzun, Jacques. *Teacher in America*. University Press of America, 1987.

37. U.S. Department of Education, National Center for Education Statistics, Integrated Postsecondary Data System (IPEDS), 'Bachelor's Degrees Awarded by Six-Digit CIP Code Among All Title IV—Eligible Institutions,' accessed on September 9, 2013

38. 'Ch 3: The Absolut Rolex Plan.' *The End of College: Creating the Future of Learning and the University of Everywhere*, by Kevin Carey, Riverhead Books, 2016.

39. Veysey, Laurence R. *The Emergence of the American University.* Univ. of Chicago Press, 1992.

40. Science, the endless frontier; a report to the President on a program for postwar scientific research. https://archive.org/stream/scienceendlessfr00unit/scienceendlessfr00unit_djvu.txt

41. John Thelin, A History of American Higher Education, Baltimore: Johns Hopkins University Press, 2004, p. 263.

42. Figure 1. Andrew Haughwout, Donghoon Lee, Joelle Scally, and Wilbert van der Klaauw, Measuring Student Debt and Its Performance (Staff Report 668, Federal Reserve Bank of New York, April 2014), https://www.newyorkfed.org/medialibrary/media/research/staff_reports/sr668.pdf

43. Rob Kuznia, 'Special Guest Bill Clinton Delivers Redondo Union High Commencement Speech,' Daily Breeze, June 14, 2012, http://www.dailybreeze.com/general-news/20120615/special-guest-bill-clinton-delivers-redondo-union-high-commencement-speech.

44. Obama, B. Speech. https://www.youtube.com/watch?v=VqSy7R_xrPY

45. 'Digest of Education Statistics, 2013.' *National Center for Education Statistics (NCES) Home Page, a Part of the U.S. Department of Education,* nces.ed.gov/programs/digest/d13/tables/dt13_302.60.asp.

46. National Center for Education Statistics (NCES), The Condition of Education, tables 20 and 233; and NCES, Digest of Educational Statistics, table 302.30.

47. 'Ch5: Who Cares If It's Signaling?' *The Case against Education: Why the Education System Is a Waste of Time and Money,* by Bryan Douglas Caplan, Princeton University Press, 2019.

48. Wall Street Journal. *Is Business School Worth It? How MBA Programs Are Revamping in 2019 | WSJ.* Youtube. Time stamp: 5:25. https://www.youtube.com/watch?v=_igXAjWIQMI

49. Miles Kimball. Bloomberg August 7, 2018. *False Advertising for College Is Pretty Much the Norm* https://www.bloomberg.com/opinion/articles/2018-08-07/for-profit-colleges-aren-t-the-only-ones-with-false-advertising

50. Chapter 4. Bet-David, Patrick, and Thomas N. Ellsworth. *Drop out and*

Get Schooled: The Case for Thinking Twice about College. Valuetainment Publishing, 2017

51. Ben Popken. Aug 6 2015. NBC. *College Textbook Prices Have Risen 1,041 Percent Since 1977.* https://www.nbcnews.com/feature/freshman-year/college-textbook-prices-have-risen-812-percent-1978-n399926. See also: Student PIRGs. Feb 3rd 2016. *Student Group Releases New Report on Textbook Prices.* https://studentpirgs.org/2016/02/03/student-group-releases-new-report-textbook-prices

52. College Kickstart. January 22nd 2018. Colleges Offering Assured/Automatic/Guaranteed Admissions. https://www.collegekickstart.com/blog/item/colleges-offering-assured-automatic-guaranteed-admissions

53. Josh Freedman. Nov 14th 2013. The Farce of Meritocracy: Why Legacy Admissions Might Actually Be A Good Thing. https://www.forbes.com/sites/joshfreedman/2013/11/14/the-farce-of-meritocracy-in-elite-higher-education-why-legacy-admissions-might-be-a-good-thing/#3f6a5c893012

54. Jaschik, S. (2016, January 21). Oberlin's president says no. Inside Higher Ed. Retrieved from https://www.insidehighered.com/news/2016/01/21/oberlins-president-refuses-negotiate-student-list-demands

55. Adler, E. (2018, March 15). Students think they can suppress speech because colleges treat them like customers. The Washington Post. Retrieved from http://wapo.st/2phMwCB?tid=ss_tw&utm_term=.75b5e44fa1d0

56. See figure 5 on page 11 of Desrochers, D. M., & Hurlburt, S. (2016, January). Trends in college spending: 2003—2013. American Institutes for Research. Delta Cost Project. Retrieved from https://www.deltacostproject.org/sites/default/files/products/15-4626%20Final01%20Delta%20Cost%20Project%20College%20Spending%2011131.406.P0.02.001%20....pdf

57. A 2013 survey by NIRSA (formerly the National Intramural-Recreational Sports Association) found ninety-two schools with pending recreation center projects totaling $1.7 billion. Cited in Rubin, C. (2014, September 19). Making a splash: College recreation now includes pool parties

and river rides. The New York Times. Retrieved from https://www.nytimes.com/2014/09/21/fashion/college-recreation-now-includes-pool-parties-and-river-rides.html. See also: Koch, J. V. (2018, January 9). Opinion: No college kid needs a water park to study. The New York Times. Retrieved from https://www.nytimes.com/2018/01/09/opinion/trustees-tuition-lazy-rivers.html

58. Carlson, S. (2013, January 28). What's the payoff for the 'country club' college? The Chronicle of Higher Education. Retrieved from https://www.chronicle.com/blogs/buildings/whats-the-payoff-for-the-country-club-college/32477 [inactive]. See also: College Ranker. (n.d.). Colleges as country clubs: Today's pampered college students. Retrieved from http://www.collegeranker.com/features/colleges-as-country-clubs. See also: Jacob, B., McCall, B. & Stange, K. M. (2013, January). College as country club: Do colleges cater to students' preferences for consumption? National Bureau of Economic Research. Retrieved from http://www.nber.org/papers/w18745.pdf. See also: Forbes poked fun at the practice by comparing colleges and country clubs to 'Club Fed' minimum-security correctional facilities. Pierce, K. (2014, July 29). College, country club or prison? Forbes. Retrieved from https://www.forbes.com/special-report/2014/country-college-prion.html

59. Open the Books, Oversight Report. March 2017. *Ivy League, Inc.* https://www.openthebooks.com/assets/1/7/Oversight_IvyLeagueInc_FINAL.pdf. See also: The Daily Pennsylvania April 12 2017. *New report shows Ivy League schools get more federal funding than some states.* https://www.thedp.com/article/2017/04/ivy-league-tax-report

60. Ewald B. Nyquist, Life Begins at Forty: A Brief History of the Commission, Middle States Association of Colleges and Schools, 1961, http://www.msche.org/documents/History-Revisited.pdf.

61. Kosslyn, Stephen M., et al. 'Higher Education in the Twenty-First Century.' *Minerva and the Future of Higher Education,* The MIT Press, 2018.

62. Sandy Baum, Jennifer Ma, and Kathleen Payea, Education Pays 2013: The Benefits of Education for Individuals and Society, College Board, 2013, p. 41, http://trends.collegeboard.org/sites/default/files/education-pays-

2013-full-report.pdf.

63. O'Keeffe, Kate. 'Education Department Investigating Harvard, Yale Over Foreign Funding.' *The Wall Street Journal*, Dow Jones & Company, 13 Feb. 2020, www.wsj.com/articles/education-department-investigating-harvard-yale-over-foreign-funding-11581539042. See also: 'U.S. Department of Education Launches Investigation into Foreign Gifts Reporting at Ivy League Universities.' *U.S. Department of Education Launches Investigation into Foreign Gifts Reporting at Ivy League Universities | U.S. Department of Education*, 12 Feb. 2020, www.ed.gov/news/press-releases/test-0

Chapter 15

1. Long, Heather. 'Is College Worth It? Goldman Sachs Says Maybe Not.' CNNMoney, Cable News Network, money.cnn.com/2015/12/09/news/economy/college-not-worth-it-goldman/index.html. See also: Roche, Julia La. 'GOLDMAN SACHS: College May Not Be Worth It.' *Business Insider*, Business Insider, 2 Dec. 2015, www.businessinsider.com/goldman-research-on-economic-return-of-college-2015-12.

2. 'Chapter 1: Why Do People with More Education Get Better Jobs?' *Will College Pay off?: a Guide to the Most Important Financial Decision You'll Ever Make*, by Peter Cappelli, PublicAffairs, 2015.

3. Christopher Caldwell, 'Live and Let Die,' Claremont Review of Books, Fall 2012, http://www.claremont.org/plublications/crb/id.1970/article_detail.asp

4. See index 2.

5. Michael Greenstone and Adam Looney, 'Where Is the Best Place to Invest $102,000—in Stocks, Bonds, or a College Degree?,' Hamilton Project, June 25, 2011, http://www.hamiltonproject.org/files/downloads_and_links/06_college_value.pdf.

6. See Louis Lavelle, 'College ROI: What We Found,' Businessweek, April 9, 2012, http://www.businessweek.com/articles/2012-04-09/college-roi-what-we-found#p2.

7. Fredro, and Gay Brennan. 'What Is Room and Board & What Will It

Cost You?' The Scholarship System, 3 Apr. 2020, thescholarshipsystem. com/blog-for-students-families/what-is-room-and-board-what-will-it-cost-you/.

8. Bok, D. (2013). *Higher education in America*. Princetn, NJ: Princeton University Press. Bowen, W. G., & McPherson, M. S. (2016). *Lesson plan: An agenda for change in American higher education*. Princeton, NJ: Princeton University Press

9. Justin D. Baer, Andrea L. Cook, and Stéphane Baldi, The Literacy of America's College Students, American Institutes for Research, 2006

10. Richard Arum and Josipa Roksa, Academically Adrift: Limited Learning on College Campuses, Chicago: University of Chicago Press, 2010.

11. OECD Skills Outlook 2013: First Results from the Survey of Adult Skills, 2013.

12. Perkins, David. 1985. 'Postprimary Education Has Little Impact on Informal Reasoning.' Journal of Educational Psychology 77 (5): 562—71.

13. Leshowitz, Barry. 1989. *'It Is Time We Did Something about Scientific Illiteracy.'* American Psychologist 44 (8): 1159—60.

14. Fain, Paul. 'Employers as Educators.' *Insidehighered*, 17 July 2019, www. insidehighered.com/digital-learning/article/2019/07/17/amazon-google-and-other-tech-companies-expand-their. See also: Blumenstyk, Goldie. 'Big Companies Are Investing in Free College. Will Their Commitments Last?' *The Chronicle of Higher Education*, The Chronicle of Higher Education, 28 Aug. 2018, www.chronicle.com/article/ Big-Companies-Are-Investing-in/244375. See also: Guthrie, Doug. 'Corporate Universities: An Emerging Threat to Graduate Business Education.' *Forbes*, Forbes Magazine, 22 Jan. 2013, www.forbes.com/ sites/dougguthrie/2013/01/22/corporate-universities-an-emerging-threat-to-graduate-business-education/#392aa33b17a0. See also: Marcus, Jon. 'Impatient With Colleges, Employers Design Their Own Courses.' *Wired*, Conde Nast, 18 Dec. 2017, www.wired.com/story/ impatient-with-colleges-employers-design-their-own-courses/.

15. See index 2.

16. U.S. Department of Education, Institute of Education Sciences, National

Center for Education Statistics, Digest of Education Statistics, 2012, Table 376.

17. U.S. Department of Education, National Center for Education Statistics, Integrated Postsecondary Data System (IPEDS) Graduation Rate Survey.

18. Lutz Berkner, Susan Choy, and Tracy Hunt-White, Descriptive Summary of 2003—04 Beginning Postsecondary Students: Three Years Later, U.S. Department of Education, National Center for Education Statistics, 2008.

19. Alexandria Walton Radford, Lutz Berkner, Sara Wheeless, and Bryan Shepherd, Persistence and Attainment of 2003—04 Beginning Postsecondary Students: After Six Years, U.S. Department of Education, National Center for Education Statistics, 2010.

20. Strayhorn, Terrell. 2010. 'Money Matters: The Influence of Financial Factors on Graduate Student Persistence.' Journal of Student Financial Aid 40 (3): 4—25. See also: Perna, Laura. 2004. 'Understanding the Decision to Enroll in Graduate School: Sex and Racial/Ethnic Group Differences.' Journal of Higher Education 75 (5): 487—527. See also: Mullen, Ann, Kimberly Goyette, and Joseph Soares. 2003. 'Who Goes to Graduate School? Social and Academic Correlates of Educational Continuation after College.' Sociology of Education 76 (2): 143—69.

21. Roser, Max, et al. 'Internet.' Our World in Data, 14 July 2015, ourworldindata.org/internet.

22. Cummings, Jozen (2005-08-29). 'Kanye West Late Registration— PopMatters Music Review'. *PopMatters*. Archived from the original on 2009-07-15.

23. http://www.high-school.devry.edu/parents.jsp. See also: Index 2.

24. For DeVry's statistics, see DeVry University, 'DeVry University Graduate Employment Statistics,' 2013, http://www.devry.edu/d/us-combined-graduates-employment-statistics.pdf.) Interestingly, in the same year, according to a non-profit research organization, The National Association of Colleges and Employers, only 6.5% Communications graduates across USA secured a job in their field. (Capelli, Ch1 Unpublished data from National Association of Colleges and Employers.

25. See index 1.

26. For more on the breakdown of training and long-term careers, see

Peter Cappelli, The New Deal at Work: Managing the Market-Driven Workforce (Boston: Harvard Business School Press, 1999)

27. References for these data are in Peter Cappelli, 'Skill Shortages, Skill Gaps, and Skill Mismatches: Evidence and Arguments for the U.S.,' ILR Review, April 2015.

28. American Presidency Project. 2015. *'Lyndon B. Johnson: 'Remarks at Southwest Texas State College upon Signing the Higher Education Act of 1965.' '* http://www.presidency.ucsb.edu/ws/?pid=27356.

29. Paul Beaudry, David A. Green, and Benjamin M. Sand, 'The Great Reversal in the Demand for Skill and Cognitive Tasks' (NBER Working Paper 18901, 2013), 3. An earlier argument suggests that the trend for college-educated men to end up in jobs that require less than a college degree started earlier. David Autor, 'The Polarization of Job Opportunities in the U.S. Labor Market: Implications for Employment and Earnings' (Washington, DC: Center for American Progress and the Hamilton Project, 2010)

30. Richard B. Freeman, 'A Cobweb Model of the Supply and Starting Salaries of New Engineers,' Industrial and Labor Relations Review 29, no. 2 (1976): 236—248.

31. See 'The Skills and Qualities Employers Value Most in Their New Hires' (press release, Bethlehem, PA, National Association of Colleges and Employers, 2014)

32. 'Chapter 5: Getting That First Job After College.' Will College Pay off?: a Guide to the Most Important Financial Decision You'll Ever Make, by Peter Cappelli, PublicAffairs, 2015.

33. Weissmann, Jordan. *'53% Of Recent College Grads Are Jobless or Underemployed-How?'* The Atlantic, Atlantic Media Company, 23 Apr. 2012, www.theatlantic.com/business/archive/2012/04/53-of-recent-college-grads-are-jobless-or-underemployed-how/256237/.

34. These results come from a survey of recent school leavers: Board of Governors of the Federal Reserve System, In the Shadow of the Great Recession: Experiences and Perspectives of Young Workers (November 2014).

35. See index 38.

36. See index 38.

37. Catherine Rampell, 'Many with New College Degrees Find Job Market Humbling,' New York Times, May 18, 2011, www.nytimes.com/2011/05/19/business/economy/19grads.html.

38. Richard Vedder, 'Why Did 17 Million Students Go to College?,' Chronicle of Higher Education, October 20, 2010, http://chronicle.com/blogs/innovations/why-did-17-million-students-go-to-college/27634

39. Team, Glassdoor. 'Google & 14 More Companies That No Longer Require a Degree.' Glassdoor Blog, 13 Jan. 2020, www.glassdoor.com/blog/no-degree-required/. See also: Editor, Joseph MilordFollowNews. 'No Degree? No Problem. Here Are the Jobs at Top Companies You Can Land without One.' *LinkedIn*, 8 Apr. 2019, www.linkedin.com/pulse/degree-problem-you-can-still-land-jobs-top-companies-joseph-milord/.

40. Youtube. The SlowMo Guys. *How a Slinky falls in Slow Motion-The Slow Mo Guys.* Aug 26, 2012. https://www.youtube.com/watch?v=rCw5JXD18y4.

41. 'The NCES Fast Facts Tool Provides Quick Answers to Many Education Questions (National Center for Education Statistics).' *National Center for Education Statistics (NCES) Home Page, a Part of the U.S. Department of Education,* nces.ed.gov/fastfacts/display.asp?id=372.

42. 'Current World Population.' *Worldometer,* www.worldometers.info/world-population/

43. Philip S. Babcock and Mindy Marks, The Falling Time Cost of College: Evidence from Half a Century of Time Use Data, National Bureau of Economic Research working paper, April 2010.

Chapter 16

1. Benjamin Bloom, 'Learning for Mastery,' *Evaluation Comment* 1, no. 2 (1968); James Block, *Mastery Learning: Theory and Practice* (New York: Holt, Rinehart & Winston, 1971)

2. T. Guskey and S. Gates, 'Synthesis of Research on the Effects of Mastery Learning in Elementary and Secondary Classrooms,' *Educational Leadership* 43, no. 8 (1986)

3. D. Levine, *Improving Student Achievement Through Mastery Learning Programs* (San Francisco: Jossey-Bass, 1985)

4. D. Davis and J. Sorrell, 'Mastery Learning in Public Schools,' *Educational Psychology Interactive* (Valdosta, GA: Valdosta State University, December 1995)

5. Freeman, S., Eddy, S. L., McDonough, M., Smith, M. K., Okoroafor, N., Jordt, H., et al. (2014). Active learning increases student performance in science, engineering, and mathematics. *Proceedings of the National Academy of Sciences of the United States of America*, 111(23), 8410-8415.

6. Dale, E. (1969). *Audiovisual methods in teaching*. New York, NY: Dryden Press

7. Bligh, D. (2000). *What's the use of lectures?* New York, NY: Jossey-Bass

8. Joan Middendorf and Alan Kalish, 'The 'Change-Up' in Lectures,' National Teaching & Learning Forum 5, no. 2 (1996).

9. 'Chapter 2: No Frill-Videos.' *The One World Schoolhouse: Education Reimagined*, by Salman Khan, Hodder & Stoughton, 2012.

10. Brooks, R., & Meltzoff, A.N. (2002). The importance of eyes, How infants interpret adult looking behavior. *Developmental Psychology*, 38, 958-966. See also: (2008). Infant gaze following and pointing predict accelerated vocabulary growth through two years of age: A longitudinal growth curve modeling study. *Journal of Child Language*, 5, 207-220.

11. 'Chapter 1: Teaching Nadia.' The One World Schoolhouse: Education Reimagined, by Salman Khan, Hodder & Stoughton, 2012.

12. Kandel, Eric R. In Search of Memory: the Emergence of a New Science of Mind. Norton & Company, 2007.

13. 'Chapter 4: Cathedrals.' The End of College: Creating the Future of Learning and the University of Everywhere, by Kevin Carey, Riverhead Books, 2016.

14. In 1973, Herbert Simon and a Carnegie Mellon psychologist named William Chase: William G. Chase and Herbert A. Simon, 'Perception in Chess,' Cognitive Psychology 4 (1973), pp. 55—81.

15. Ericsson, K. A., Chase, W. G., & Faloon, S. (1980). Acquisition of a memory skill. *Science, 208*(4448), 1181-1182.

16. Heath, Chip, and Dan Heath. Made to Stick: Why Some Ideas Survive

and Others Die. Random House, 2010.

17. 'Chapter 10: Tests and Testing.' The One World Schoolhouse: Education Reimagined, by Salman Khan, Hodder & Stoughton, 2012.

18. 'Chapter 1: What Have We Done To Childhood?' Free to Learn: Why Unleashing the Instinct to Play Will Make Our Children Happier, More Self-Reliant, and Better Students for Life, by Peter Gray, Basic Books, 2015.

19. Adair, R., Eyerman, R., Harms,R., Howe, R., J., et al. (2014, February). Report to Dean Mary Miller from the Ad Hoc Committee on Grading. New Haven: Yale College. http://yalecollege.yale.edu/site/defaullt/files/files/gradingreport201402.pdf)

20. Cited in: Babcock, Phillip & Marks, Mindy. (2010). Leisure College, Usa. Department of Economics, UC Santa Barbara, University of California at Santa Barbara, Economics Working Paper Series.

21. See Phillip L. Roth, Craig A. BeVier, Fred S. Switzer III, and Jeffery S. Schippman, 'Meta-Analyzing the Relations Between Grades and Job Performance,' Journal of Applied Psychology 81, no. 5 (1996): 548—556.

22. Youtube. *Brown eyes and blue eyes Racism experiment Children Session - Jane Elliott.* https://www.youtube.com/watch?v=oGvoXeXCoUYs

23. Hacking, I. (1991). The making and molding of child abuse. Critical Inquiry, 17, 253—288. As described in: Haslam, N. (2016). Concept creep: Psychology's expanding concepts of harm and pathology. Psychological Inquiry, 27(1), 1—17

24. Khan, Sal, director. *Let's Use Video to Reinvent Education.* TED, Mar. 2011, www.ted.com/talks/sal_khan_let_s_use_video_to_reinvent_education?language=en#t-876458.

25. See index 17.

26. Gray, P. (2009). Play as the foundation for hunter-gatherer social existence. *American Journal of Play, 1,* 476-552

27. Konner, M. (1975). Relations amongst infants and juveniles in comparative perspective. In M. Lewis & L. A. Rosenblum (Eds.). *The origins of behaviour, vol. 4: Friendship and peer relations,* 99-129. New York: Wiley

28. Vygotsky, L. (1978). Interaction between learning and development. In

M. Cole, V. John-Steiner, S. Scribner, and E.Souberman (Eds.), *Mind and society: The development of higher psychological processes*. Cambridge, MA: Harvard University Press

29. Wood, D. J., Bruner, J. S., & Ross, G. (1976). The role of tutoring in problem solving. *Journal of Clinical Psychiatry*, 17, 89-100

30. Emfinger, K. (2009). Numerical conceptions reflected during multi age child-initiated pretend play. *Journal of Instructional Psychology*, 36, 326-334.

31. Whiting, B. B. (1983). The genesis of prosocial behavior. In D. L. Bridgman (Ed.), *The nature of prosocial development: Interdisciplinary theories and strategies*, 221-242. New York: Academic Press

32. 'Part 3: Into the Real World' The One World Schoolhouse: Education Reimagined, by Salman Khan, Hodder & Stoughton, 2012.

33. 'Chapter 6: The Human Educative Instincts.' Free to Learn: Why Unleashing the Instinct to Play Will Make Our Children Happier, More Self-Reliant, and Better Students for Life, by Peter Gray, Basic Books, 2015.

34. 'Chapter 7: The Playful State of Mind.' Free to Learn: Why Unleashing the Instinct to Play Will Make Our Children Happier, More Self-Reliant, and Better Students for Life, by Peter Gray, Basic Books, 2015.

35. Isen, A. M., Daubman, K. A., & Nowicki, G. P. (1987) Positive affect facilitates creative problem solving. *Journal of Personality and Social Psychology*, 52, 112-1131

36. Richards, C. A., & Sandersoon, J. A. (1999). The role of imagination in facilitating deductive reasoning in 2-, 3-, and 4-year-olds. *Cognition*, 72, 81-89

37. 'Chapter 7: The Playful State of Mind.' Free to Learn: Why Unleashing the Instinct to Play Will Make Our Children Happier, More Self-Reliant, and Better Students for Life, by Peter Gray, Basic Books, 2015.

38. Hofferth, S. L., & Sandberg, J. F. (2001). Changes in American children's time, 1981-1997. In T. Owens & S. L. Hofferth (Eds.), *Children at the millenium: Where have we come from, where are we going?* 193-229. New York: Elsevier Science

39. Hofferth, S. (2009). Changes in American children's time, 1997-2003.

International Journal of Time Use Research, 6, 26-47

40. Yazzie-Mintz, Ethan. 2010. Charting the Path from Engagement to Achievement: A Report on the 2009 High School Survey of Student Engagement. Bloomington, IN: Center for Evaluation and Education Policy. http://ceep.indiana.edu/hssse/images/HSSSE_2010_Report.pdf

41. Larson, Reed, and Maryse Richards. 1991. 'Boredom in the Middle School Years: Blaming Schools versus Blaming Students.' American Journal of Education 99 (4): 418—43

42. Bridgeland, John, John DiIulio Jr., and Karen Morison. 2006. The Silent Epidemic: Perspectives of High School Dropouts. Washington, DC: Civic Enterprises. http://files.eric.ed.gov/fulltext/ED513444.pdf.

43. Mann, Sandi, and Andrew Robinson. 2009. 'Boredom in the Lecture Theatre: An Investigation into the Contributors, Moderators and Outcomes of Boredom amongst University Students.' British Educational Research Journal 35 (2): 243—58

44. Romer, David. 1993. 'Do Students Go to Class? Should They?' Journal of Economic Perspectives 7 (3): 167—74

45. Pinker, Steven. 2014. 'The Trouble with Harvard: The Ivy League Is Broken and Only Standardized Tests Can Fix It.' New Republic. September 4. http://www.newrepublic.com/article/119321/harvard-ivy-league-should-judge-students-standardized-tests.

Chapter 17

1. The Montessori School Internationale. The Method. http://themontessorischoolinternationale.com/the-montessori-method.

2. 'How It Works.' How It Works—About Us—Big Picture Learning, www.bigpicture.org/apps/pages/index.jsp?uREC_ID=389353&type=d&pREC_ID=882356.

3. 'BPL INTERNATIONAL.' BPL INTERNATIONAL - District Departments - Big Picture Learning, www.bigpicture.org/apps/pages/international.

Chapter 18

1. Faulconer, Jeanne. 'From School to Homeschool: What Is Deschooling?' TheHomeSchoolMom, 4 Mar. 2014, www.thehomeschoolmom.com/school-homeschool-what-is-deschooling/.

2. Sareen, Ayushi. 'These 10 Countries Offer Free Education To International Students. Time To Pack Your Bags!' *Top 10 Countries That Offer Free Education To International Students*, ScoopWhoop, 26 Mar. 2020, www.scoopwhoop.com/These-10-Countries-Offer-Free-Education-To-International-Students-Time-To-Pack-Your-Bags/. See also: Goetz, Lisa. '5 Countries With Virtually Free College Tuition.' *Investopedia*, Investopedia, 6 Apr. 2020, www.investopedia.com/articles/personal-finance/080616/6-countries-virtually-free-college-tuition.asp. See also: Tucker, Laura. 'Where Can You Study Abroad for Free?' *Top Universities*, 12 Feb. 2020, www.topuniversities.com/student-info/studying-abroad/where-can-you-study-abroad-free.

3. Taleb, Nassim Nicholas. *Antifragile: Things That Gain from Disorder.* Random House, 2016.

4. Ovens, Sam. 'Cause & Effect Timeframes: Why Today's Results Came From Last Years Work.' Consulting.com, www.consulting.com/channel/cause-effect-timeframes-why-todays-results-came-from-last-years-work.

5. C. S. Dweck, *Self-Theories: Their Role in Motivation, Personality, and Development* (Philadelphia: Psychology Press/Taylor & Francis, 1999)

6. Harari, Yuval Noah. *21 Lessons for the 21st Century.* Spiegel & Grau, 2018.

7. Harari, Yuval Noah. '*Yuval Noah Harari: the Myth of Freedom.*' The Guardian, Guardian News and Media, 14 Sept. 2018, www.theguardian.com/books/2018/sep/14/yuval-noah-harari-the-new-threat-to-liberal-democracy.

8. '*Bill Gates and Warren Buffett: Student Q&A 2017*'. Investors Archives. Youtube. May 23 2017. https://www.youtube.com/watch?v=1CCcheNC1sw.

9. Newton, Isaac. 'Letter from Sir Isaac Newton to Robert Hooke'. Historical Society of Pennsylvania. Retrieved 7 June 2018

10. Allen, M. (2017, November 9). Sean Parker unloads on Facebook: 'God only knows what it's doing to our children's brains.' Axios. Retrieved from https://www.axios.com/sean-parker-unloads-on-facebook-god-only-knows-what-its-doing-to-our-childrens-brains-1513306792-f855e7b4-4e99-4d60-8d51-2775559c2671.html)

11. Mischel, W, et al. *'Cognitive and Attentional Mechanisms in Delay of Gratification.'* Journal of Personality and Social Psychology, U.S. National Library of Medicine, Feb. 1972, www.ncbi.nlm.nih.gov/pubmed/5010404.

12. Mischel, W, et al. 'Delay of Gratification in Children.' *Science (New York, N.Y.),* U.S. National Library of Medicine, 26 May 1989, www.ncbi.nlm.nih.gov/pubmed/2658056. See also: Mischel, W, et al. 'The Nature of Adolescent Competencies Predicted by Preschool Delay of Gratification.' *Journal of Personality and Social Psychology,* U.S. National Library of Medicine, Apr. 1988, www.ncbi.nlm.nih.gov/pubmed/3367285. See also: Shoda, Yuichi, et al. 'Predicting Adolescent Cognitive and Self-Regulatory Competencies From Preschool Delay of Gratification: Identifying Diagnostic Conditions: Request PDF.' *ResearchGate,* www.researchgate.net/publication/232585605_Predicting_Adolescent_Cognitive_and_Self-Regulatory_Competencies_From_Preschool_Delay_of_Gratification_Identifying_Diagnostic_Conditions.

13. 'A Quote from The Demon-Haunted World.' *Goodreads,* Goodreads, www.goodreads.com/quotes/538156-there-are-naive-questions-tedious-questions-ill-phrased-questions-questions-put.